PIANO SHEET MUSIC FOR KIDS

CHARLOTTE GIBBS

© Copyright 2023 - All rights reserved.

The content contained within this book may not be reproduced, duplicated or transmitted without direct written permission from the author or the publisher.

Under no circumstances will any blame or legal responsibility be held against the publisher, or author, for any damages, reparation, or monetary loss due to the information contained within this book, either directly or indirectly.

Legal Notice:

This book is copyright protected. It is only for personal use. You cannot amend, distribute, sell, use, quote or paraphrase any part, or the content within this book, without the consent of the author or publisher.

Disclaimer Notice:

Please note the information contained within this document is for educational and entertainment purposes only. All effort has been executed to present accurate, up to date, reliable, complete information. No warranties of any kind are declared or implied. Readers acknowledge that the author is not engaged in the rendering of legal, financial, medical or professional advice. The content within this book has been derived from various sources. Please consult a licensed professional before attempting any techniques outlined in this book.

By reading this document, the reader agrees that under no circumstances is the author responsible for any losses, direct or indirect, that are incurred as a result of the use of the information contained within this document, including, but not limited to, errors, omissions, or inaccuracies.

TABLE OF CONTENTS

INTRODUCTION	5
HOW TO USE THIS BOOK	7
CHAPTER 1	15
HOT CROSS BUNS	17
BOIL THEM CABBAGE DOWN	18
BOW WOW WOW	20
IT'S RAINING, IT'S POURING	21
A- TISKET, A- TASKET	23
HUSH LITTLE BABY, DON'T YOU CRY	24
NAUGHTY KITTY CAT	26
BAA, BAA, BLACK SHEEP	28
OLD MACDONALD HAD A FARM	30
THIS OLD MAN	32
CHAPTER 2	35
OVER IN THE MEADOW	38
LAVENDER'S BLUE	42
SEE-SAW, MARGERY DAW	45
ROW, ROW, ROW YOUR BOAT	47
ARE YOU SLEEPING?	48
THERE'S A HOLE IN MY BUCKET	50
HARK, HARK! THE DOGS DO BARK	52
ST. PAUL'S STEEPLE	54
FROG WENT A-COURTIN'	58
ON TOP OF OLD SMOKEY	60
CHAPTER 3	63
POLLY WOLLY DOODLE	66
I HAD A LITTLE NUT TREE	70
B-I-N-G-O	72
THE FARMER IN THE DELL	76
HEAD, SHOULDERS, KNEES AND TOES	78
POLLY PUT THE KETTLE ON	80

MULBERRY BUSH	82
HICKORY DICKORY DOCK	84
POP GOES THE WEASEL	86
HEY DIDDLE DIDDLE	88

CHAPTER 4   91

RIG A JIG JIG	94
FIVE LITTLE DUCKS	98
ITSY BITSY SPIDER	100
HAPPY & YOU KNOW IT, CLAP YOUR HANDS	102
LONDON BRIDGE	106
BLOW THE MAN DOWN	108
ORANGES AND LEMONS	110
THE MORE WE GET TOGETHER	114
THE MUFFIN MAN	116
ROCK-A-BYE BABY	120

CHAPTER 5   123

SING A SONG OF SIXPENCE	126
ANIMAL FAIR	128
A JOLLY FAT FROG LIVED IN THE RIVER	132
RING AROUND THE ROSIES	136
YANKEE DOODLE	138
MICHAEL FINNEGAN	142
CLEMENTINE (OH MY DARLIN' CLEMENTINE)	144
BUFFALO GALS, WON'T YOU COME OUT TONIGHT	148
JOHN JACOB JINGLEHEIMER SCHMIDT	152
MY GRANDFATHER'S CLOCK	156

CONCLUSION   161

INTRODUCTION

Hello again, future piano stars! It's Tempo the Turtle here, and I'm thrilled to guide you through this new piano adventure with our fresh collection of songs just for you!

In this book, you'll find a fantastic selection of piano pieces designed especially for kids. We'll start with some easy, fun songs that will help you get comfortable with your piano keys. As you grow more confident and skilled, we'll gradually move on to slightly more challenging tunes. Don't worry, though—I'll be right here with helpful tips and friendly suggestions to make every step a breeze.

Remember, learning piano is like a journey, and we'll make sure it's full of exciting discoveries and joyful moments. Take your time, have fun, and know that every practice session brings you closer to becoming a piano master!

Ready to dive in? Let's make some beautiful music together, one note at a time. I'm here to support you every step of the way, so let's get started and enjoy the melody of learning!

HOW TO USE THIS BOOK

HOW TO SIT AND PLACE YOUR HANDS
How you sit is very important when playing piano! If you want to sit and hold your hands correctly when playing piano, this is what you need to remember:

★ Straight back.
★ Elbows at your sides without touching your body.
★ Rest your feet flat on the floor near the pedals.
★ Make sure that the bench is the right height.
★ Sit towards the edge of the bench to rest your feet on the floor or on a stool.
★ Keep your fingers curved, and use only the tips to play.

WHITE KEYS AND BLACK KEYS
The white keys are different music notes. They're named after the first seven letters of the alphabet, in this order: C, D, E, F, G, A, and B.

The black keys make the white keys sound lower or higher. They come in groups of two and groups of three keys.

The most important key is the middle C. It's in the middle of the keyboard, to the left of a group of two black keys.

FINGER NUMBERS
Finger numbers help us know which finger to use to play each key. Here's how it works for both of your hands:

★ Your thumbs are number 1.
★ Your index fingers are number 2.

★ Your middle fingers are number 3.
★ Your ring fingers are number 4.
★ And your pinky fingers are number 5.

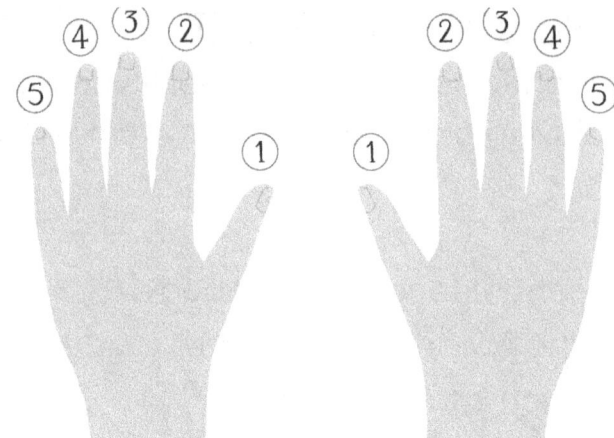

There are two ways in which you can place your hands on the keyboard. Let's take a look!

The middle C position
Rest your thumbs on middle C and place each finger on the next white key, placing both hands in the middle of the keyboard.

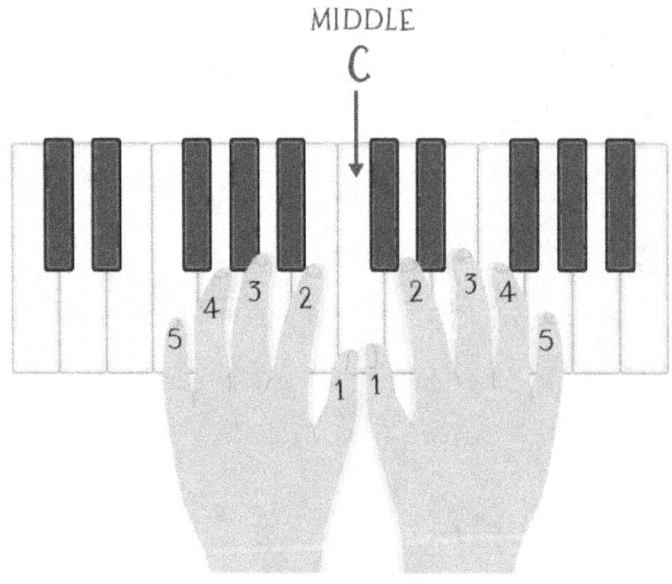

If you look at your right hand:

- ★ Your number 1 finger will be on C.
- ★ Number 2 will be on D.
- ★ Number 3 will be on E.
- ★ Number 4 will be on F.
- ★ And number 5 will be on G.

But what about A and B? You can play them with your number 5 finger by spreading your fingers or moving your hand to that side.

The C position
Another way to place your hands is called the C position. Why? Because both hands rest on a C note! They are not both on middle C this time.

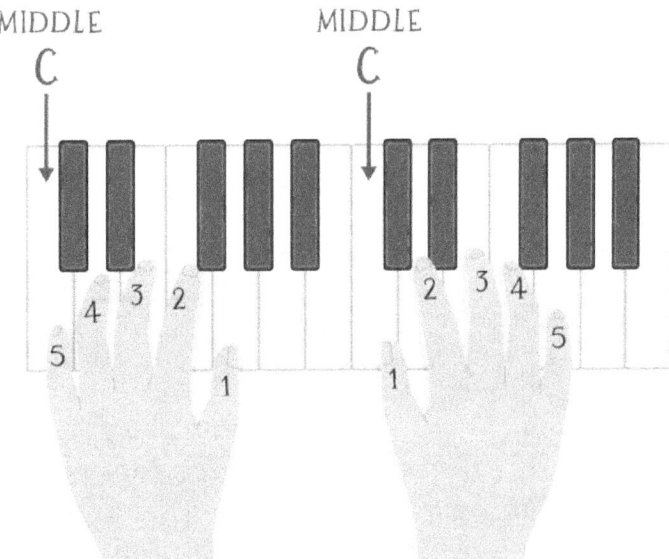

You can see that your right thumb rests on middle C, and your left pinky rests on the first C note on the left side.

But wait! What about black keys? They come in groups of two and three keys, so this is the easiest way to play them:

★ Use fingers 2 and 3 for the groups of two keys.
★ Use fingers 2, 3, and 4 for the groups of three keys.

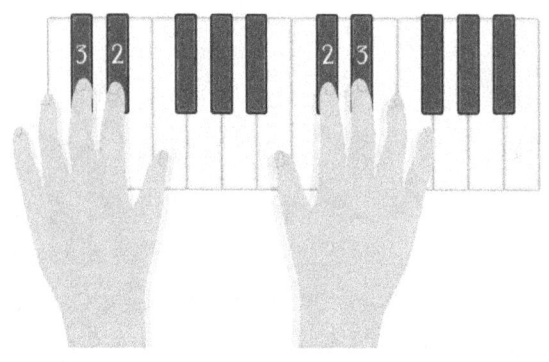

Learning key names and finger numbers can take some time. Here are two tips to make it easier:

1) Put a sticker on each key with its letter.
2) Write the number on your fingers with a washable marker!

NOTES AND RESTS

Notes are special symbols that tell us what sounds to play on the piano and for how long:

Whole notes
4 beats

Half notes
2 beats

Quarter notes
1 beat

Eight notes
Half a beat

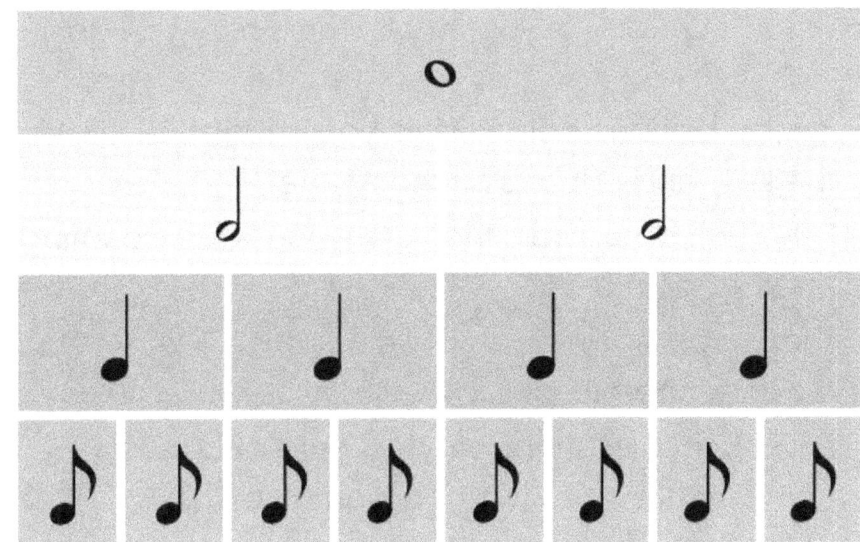

And rests are symbols that tell us when to take a break while playing the piano and for how long:

Whole rests
4 beats

Half rests
2 beats

Quarter rests
1 beat

Eighth notes
Half a rest

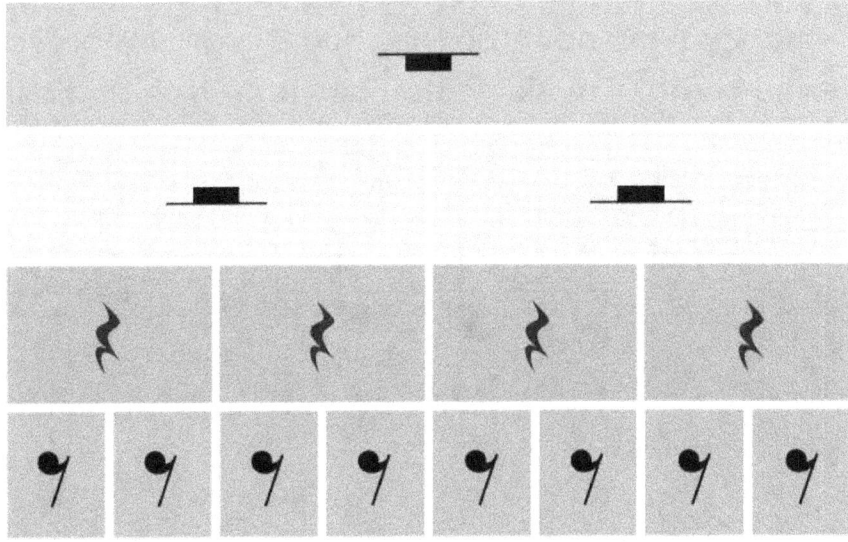

COUNTING BEATS

There are many different ways to count beats. Counting numbers, clapping, tapping on the floor... Let's keep it simple and count beats out loud until you get used to count only in your head. This is how you do it:

★ Press a key and hold it while you count 1-2-3-4. When you reach 4, let go of the key, and... that's a whole note!

★ For a half note, press that key twice while counting 1-2-3-4. Press it on 1 and press it again on 3.

★ Then, press it four times while counting 1-2-3-4. Once for each number, that's a quarter note!

★ Last but not least: the shortest note of all! Press the key twice for each number to see how fast an eighth note is.

When you count rests, you repeat the same process but without playing any keys, because they are silent!

MUSIC SHEETS, STAFFS AND CLEFS

You will be seeing a lot of these in this book! Music sheets are full of lines, notes, and fancy symbols. Those lines come in groups of five called a staff. Those staffs are the home of music notes. Each note lives on a different floor:

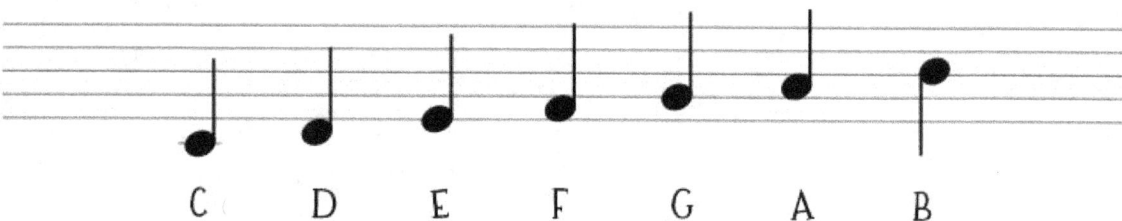

The most important fancy symbols are the clefs:

★ The treble clef tells you to play the higher notes on the right side of the keyboard. You have to play them with your right hand.

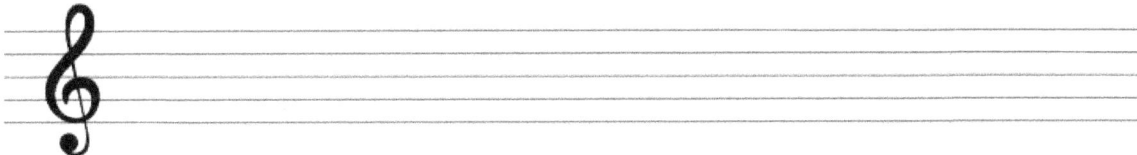

★ The bass clef tells you to play the lower notes on the left side of the keyboard. You have to play them with your left hand.

Next to the treble clef and the bass clef you will see two numbers. These are numbers that tell you important things about music. The number above tells you how many beats (counts) there are in each bear. The number below tells you what kind of beats they are.

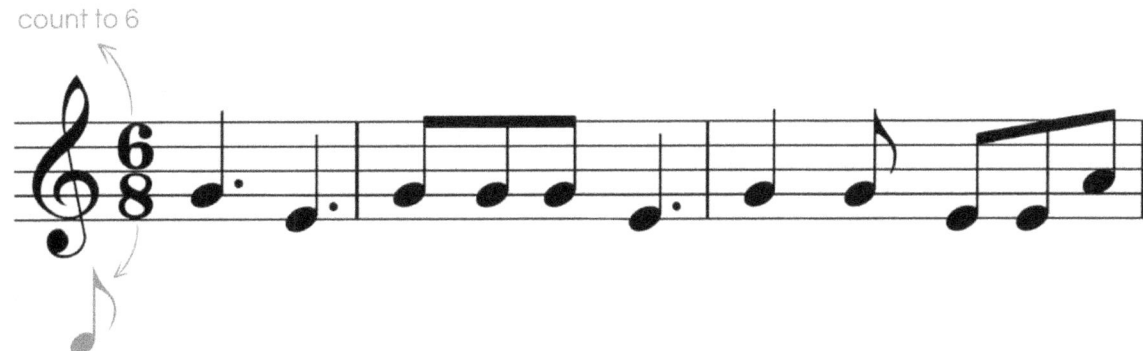

For example, if you see a number 6 above and a number 8 below, it means you count to six and each count is as quick as an eighth note. This helps you play the song at the right speed.

Alright, my friend. Now that we have reviewed the basics of piano, you are ready to put everything together and play a lot of songs!

And don't worry, I'll be with you every step of the way, with tips and trick to help you become a piano master!

CHAPTER 1

Welcome to our first chapter, where you'll discover 10 easy songs designed to make your piano practice fun and exciting as you start your musical journey!

Remember you'll play these songs with your right hand!

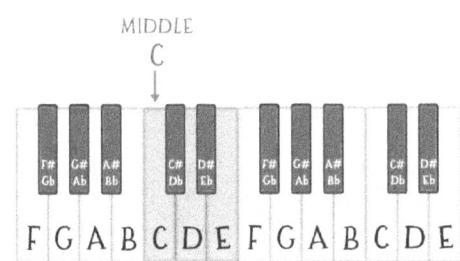
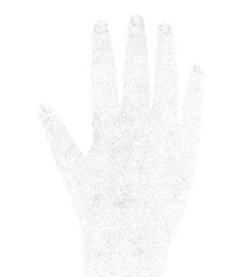

HOT CROSS BUNS

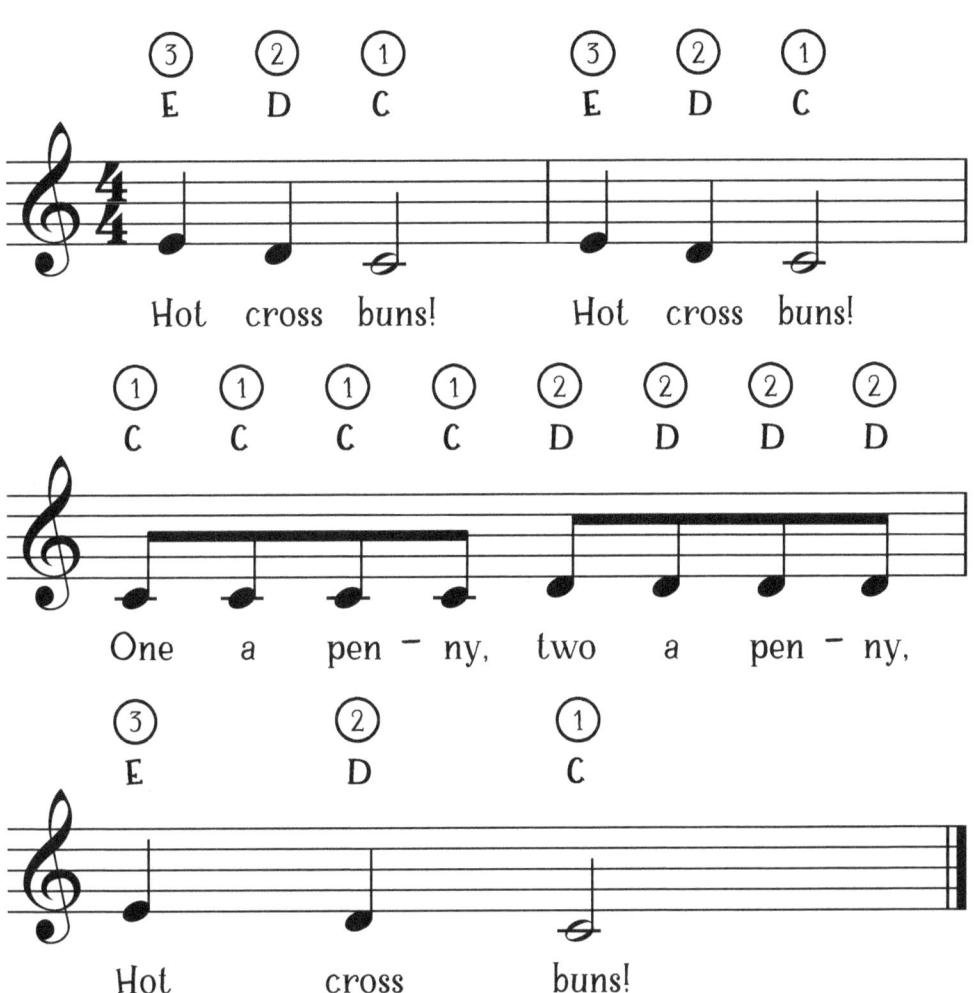

MIDDLE
C
F# Gb G# Ab A# Bb C# Db D# Eb F# Gb G# Ab A# Bb C# Db D# Eb
F G A B C D E F G A B C D E

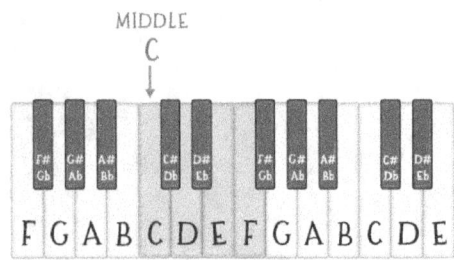

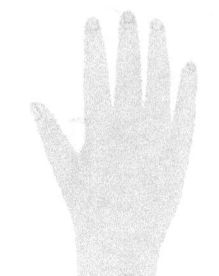

BOIL THEM CABBAGE DOWN

Refrain
3 3 3 3 4 4
E E E E F F
Boil them cab – bage down, down.
3 3 3 3 2
E E E E D
Turn them hoe – cakes 'round,
3 3 3 3 4 4 4 4
E E E E F F F F
The only song that I can sing is
3 3 2 2 1
E E D D C
Boil them cab – bage down.

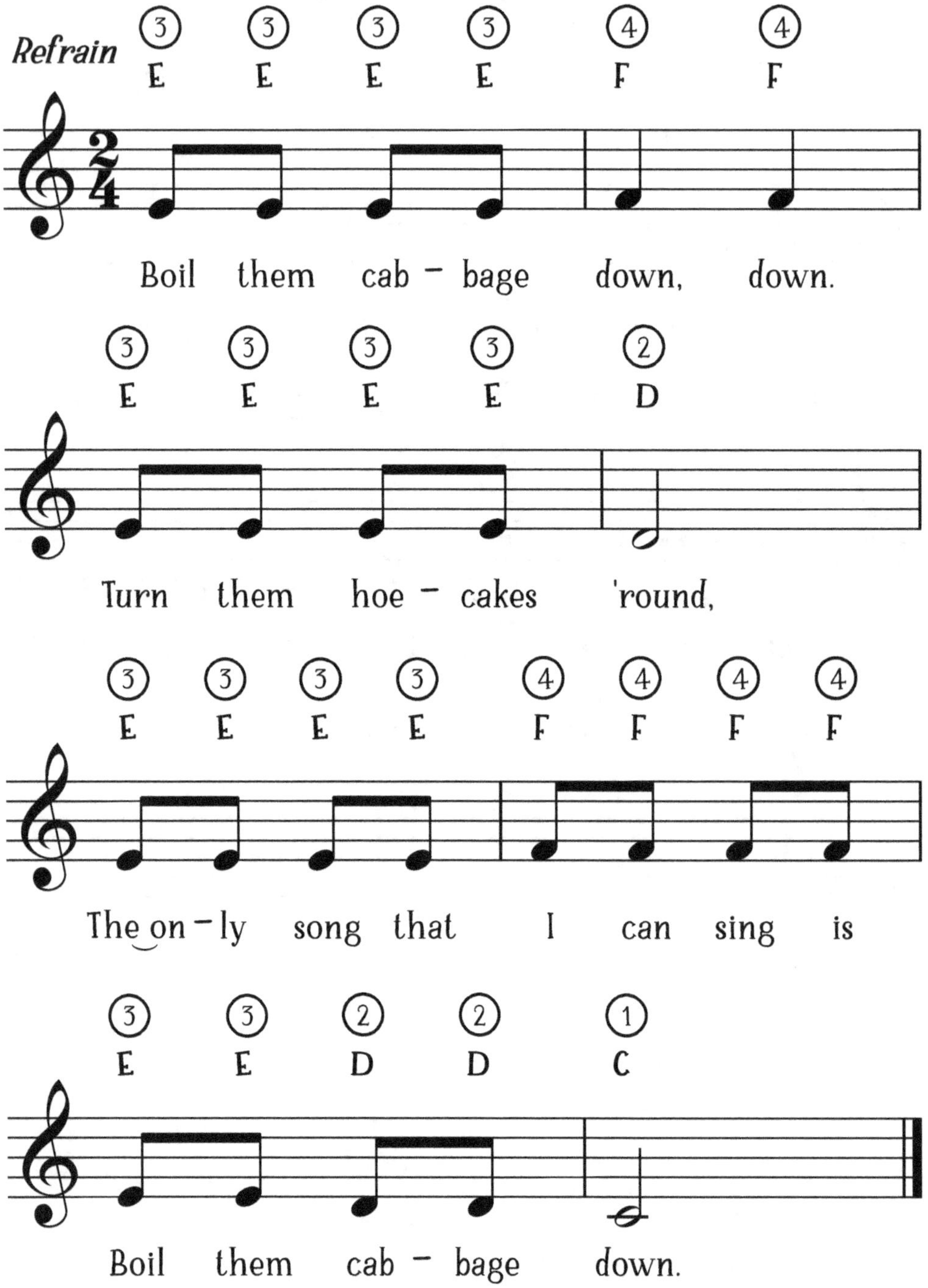

2

2. Raccoon has a bushy tail
   Possum's tail is bare
   Rabbit's got no tail at all
   But a little bunch of hair.
   Refrain

3. Someone stole my old coon dog.
   Wish they'd bring him back.
   He chased the big hogs through the fence,
   And the little ones through the crack.
   Refrain

4. Met a possum in the road,
   Blind as he could be.
   Jumped the fence and whipped my dog
   And bristled up at me.
   Refrain

5. Possum up a 'simmon tree
   Raccoon on the ground
   Raccoon say to the possum
   "Won't you shake them 'simmons down?"
   Refrain

6. Butterfly, he has wings of gold.
   Firefly, wings of flame.
   Bedbug, he got no wings at all,
   But he gets there just the same.
   Refrain

7. Once I had an old grey mule,
   his name was Simon Slick.
   He'd roll his eyes, and back his ears,
   and how that mule would kick.
   Refrain

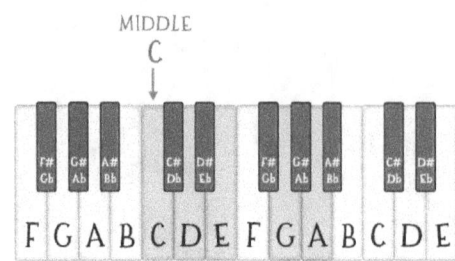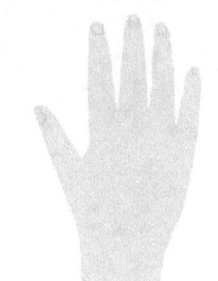

BOW WOW WOW

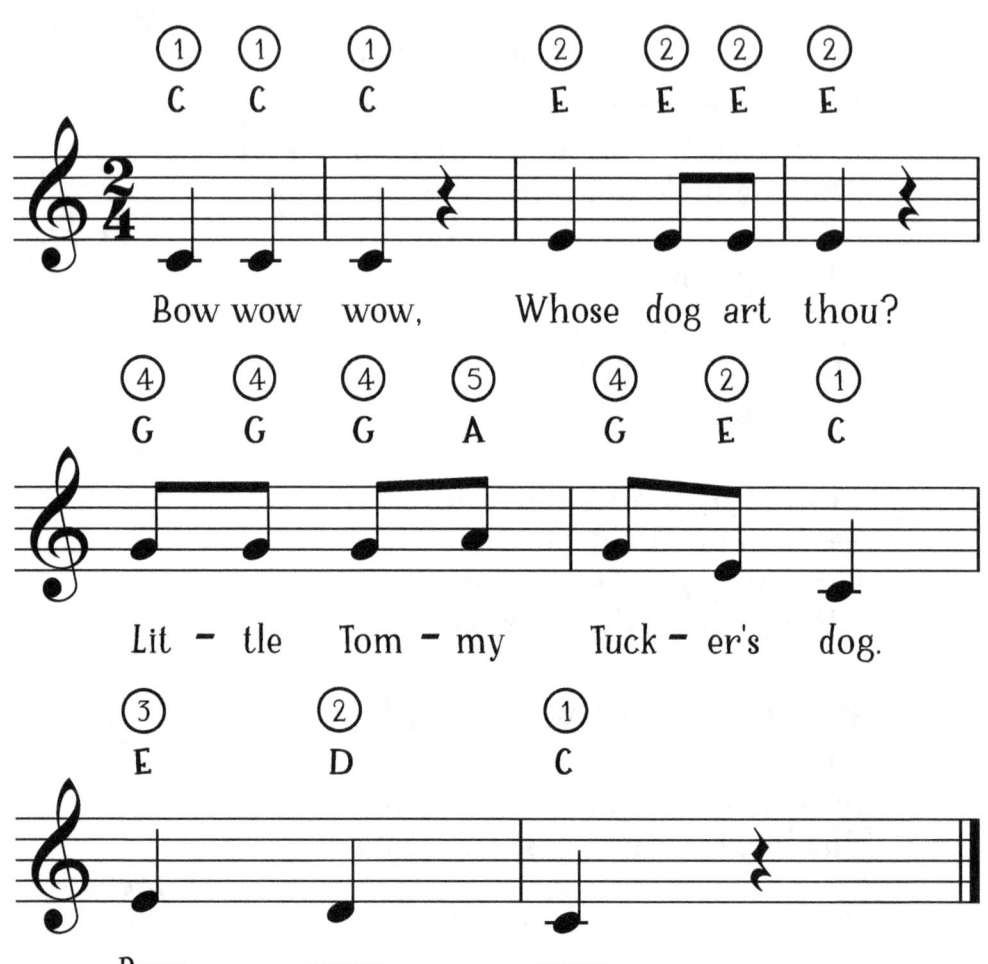

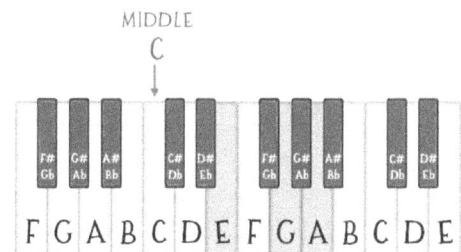

Helpful tip at the end of the song!

IT'S RAINING

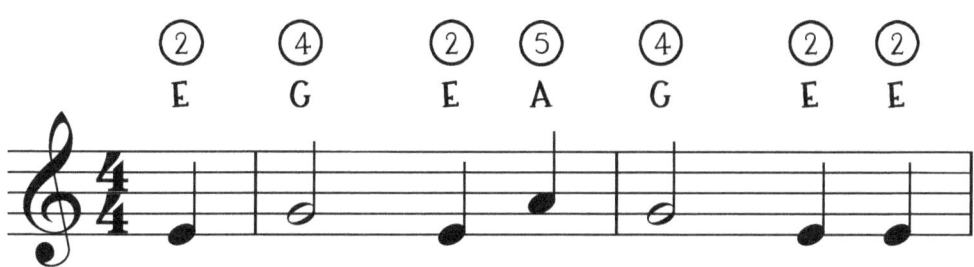

It's rain - ing, it's pour - ing, the

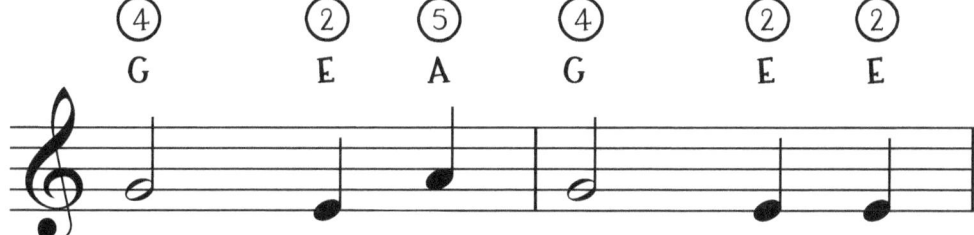

old man is snor - ing. He

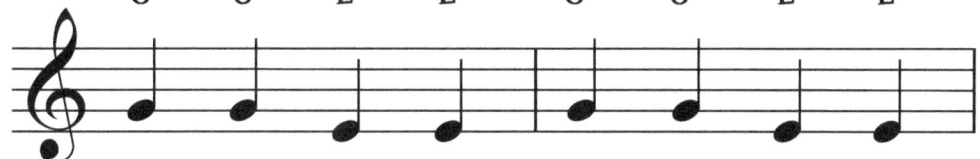

went to bed and bumped his head and

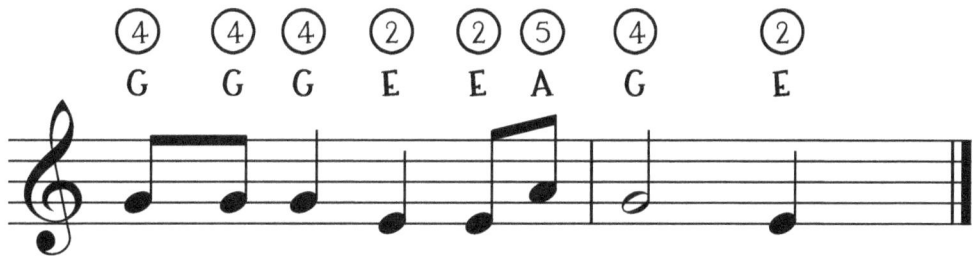

could-n't get up in the morn - ing.

Look closely at the numbers near the clef—like 4/4—and at the first bar. It might look like something's missing since there's only one note. Now check the last bar. Are there enough notes for 4/4? Not yet?

But if you add the notes from the first and last bars together, you get the right amount! That's because the first note was "borrowed" from the last bar and placed at the beginning. This means you should play the first note softly. To help, try singing the song with the words. You'll see that the music and lyrics match up perfectly!

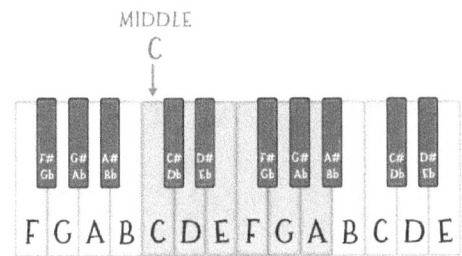
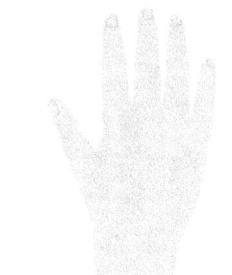

A TISKET A TASKET

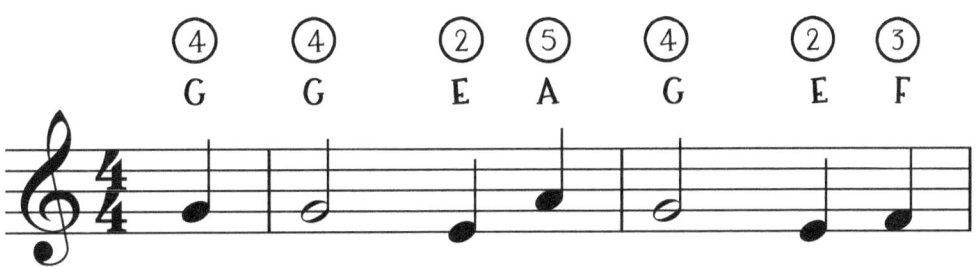

A tisk - et, a task - et, a

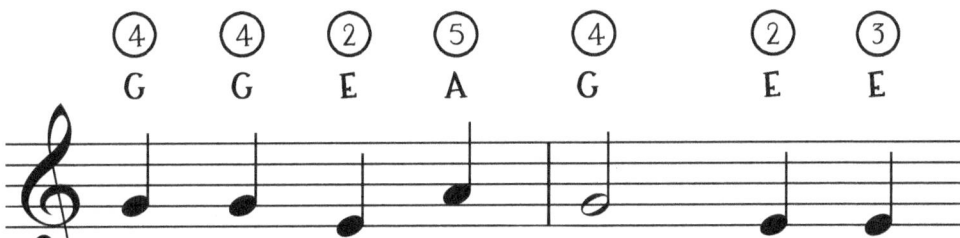

green and yel - low bask - et, I

wrote a let - ter to my friend and

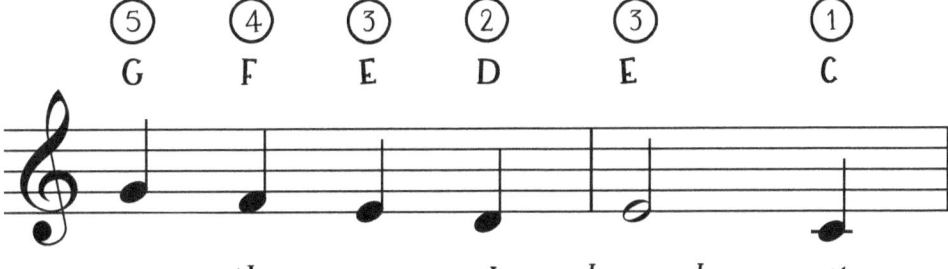

on the way I dropped it.

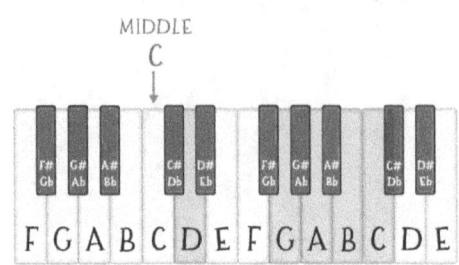

HUSH LITTLE BABY

If that mockingbird don't sing,
Mama's gonna buy you a diamond ring.

If that diamond ring turns brass,
Mama's gonna buy you a looking glass.

If that looking glass gets broke,
Mama's gonna buy you a billy-goat.

2

If that billy-goat don't pull,
Mama's gonna buy you a cart and bull.

If that cart and bull turn over,
Mama's gonna buy you a dog named Rover.

If that dog named Rover don't bark,
Mama's gonna buy you a horse and cart.

If that horse and cart fall down,
You'll still be the sweetest little baby in town.

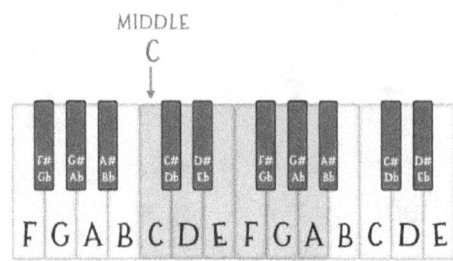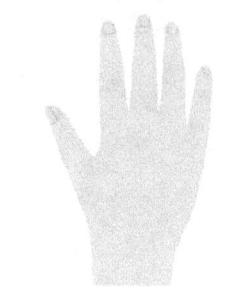

NAUGHTY KITTY CAT

Naugh - ty kit - ty cat,

You are ve - ry fat,

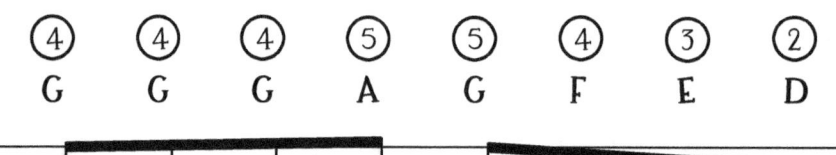

You have but - ter on your whis - kers,

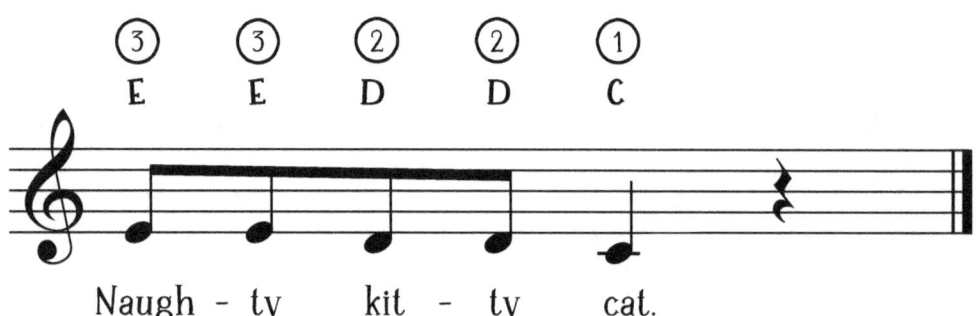

Naugh - ty kit - ty cat.

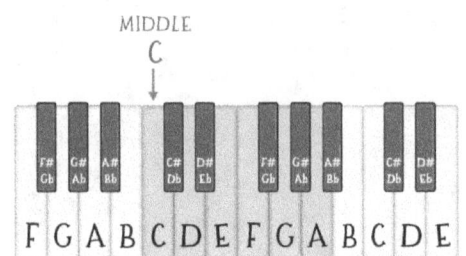 

BAA BAA BLACK SHEEP

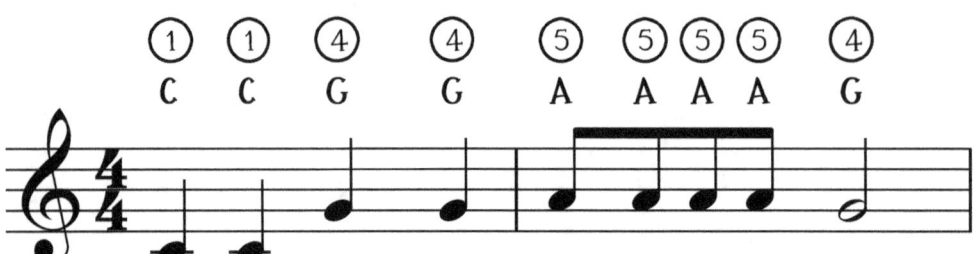

MIDDLE
C
F# Gb
G# Ab
A# Bb
C# Db
D# Eb
F# Gb
G# Ab
A# Bb
C# Db
D# Eb
F G A B C D E F G A B C D E

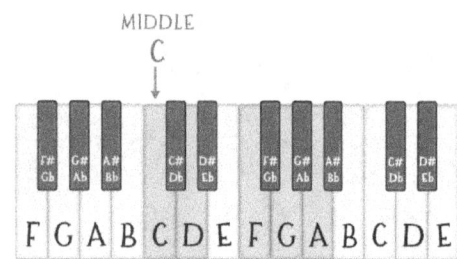

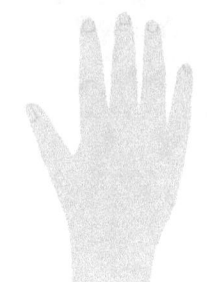

OLD MACDONALD HAD A FARM

4 4 4 1 2 2 1
F F F C D D C
Old Mac - Do - nald had a farm
5 5 4 4 3 1
A A G G F C
Ee i ee i oh. And
4 4 4 1 2 2 1
F F F C D D C
on that farm he had some cows
5 5 4 4 3 1 1
A A G G F C C
Ee i ee i oh. With a

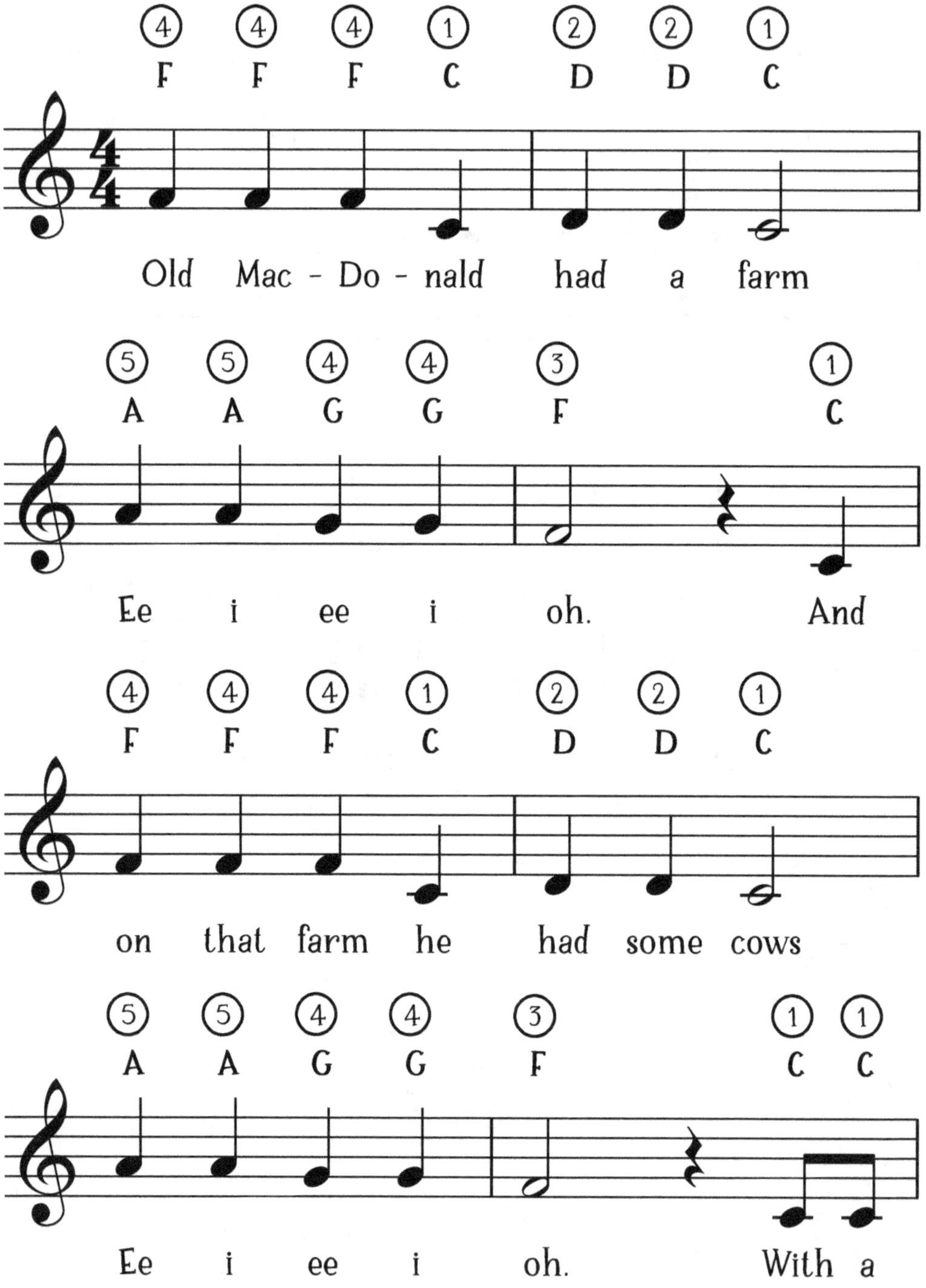

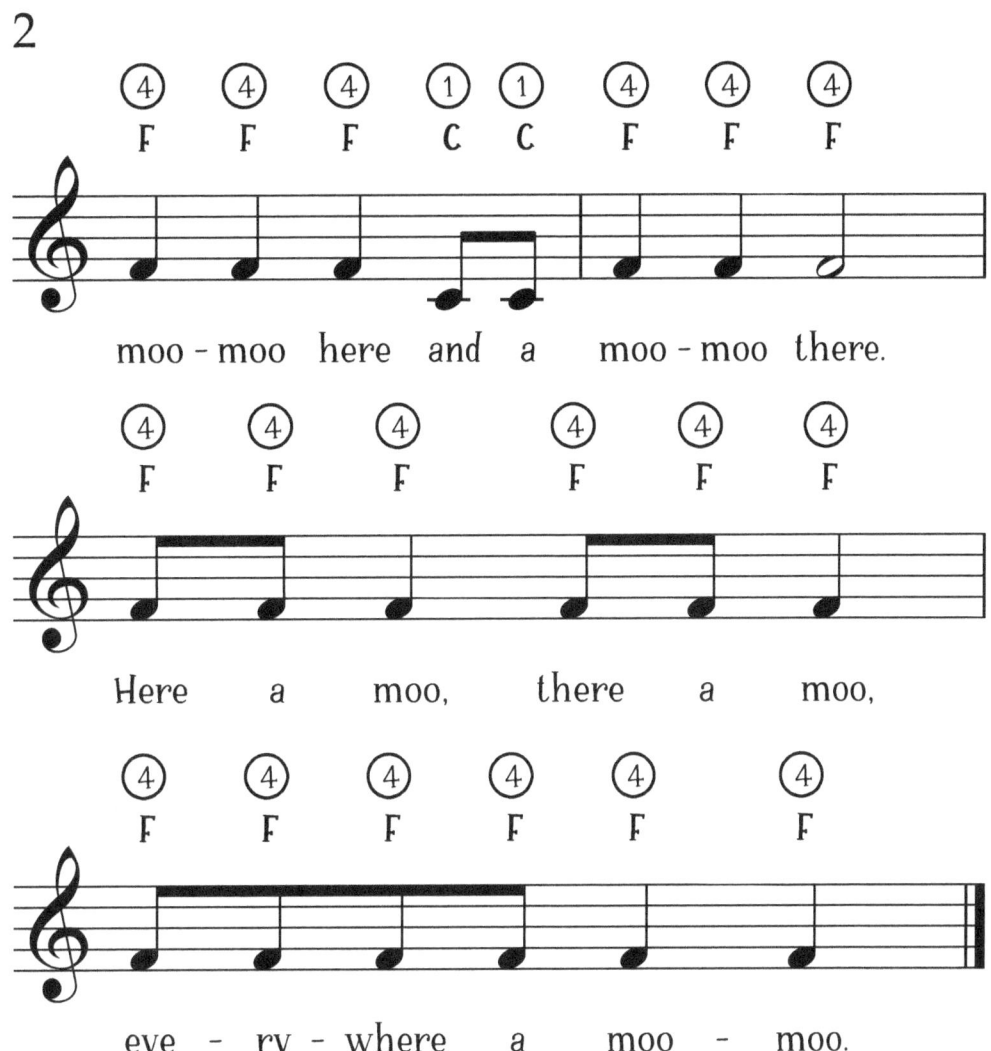

2. Chickens - cluck cluck
3. Sheep - baa baa
4. Pigs - oink oink
5. Ducks - quack quack

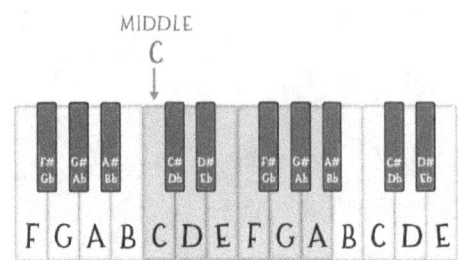

THIS OLD MAN

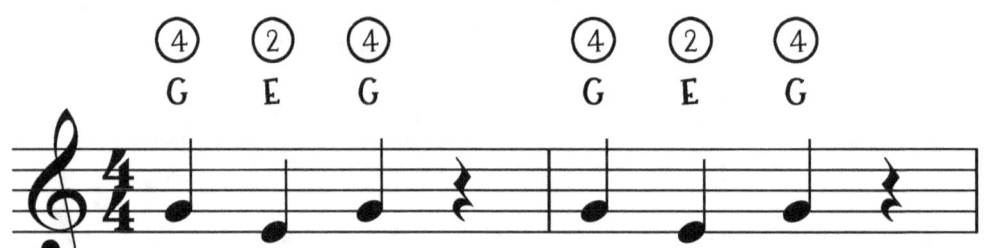

This old man, he played one,

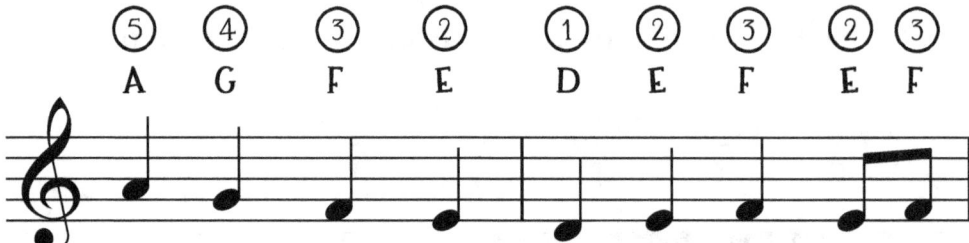

He played knick knack on my drum, with a

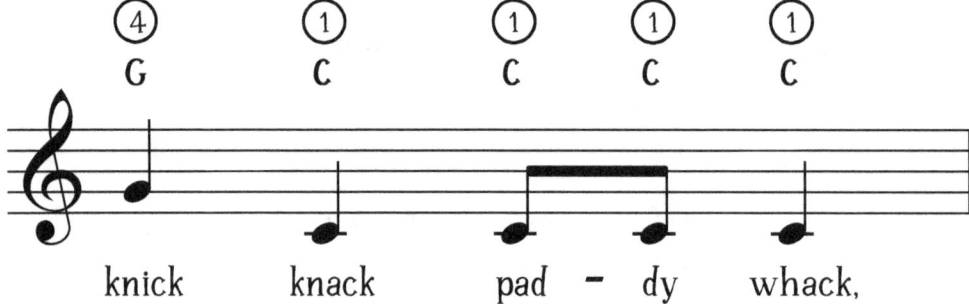

knick knack pad - dy whack,

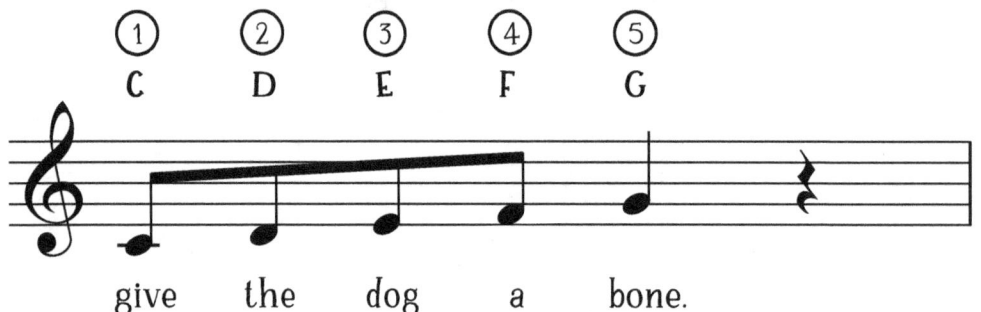

give the dog a bone.

2

This old man came rol-ling home.

This old man, he played two,
He played "knick knack" on my shoe...
... three ... knee ...
... four ... door ...
... five ... hive ...
... six ... sticks ...
... seven ... up to heaven ...
... eight ... gate ...
... nine ... vine ...
... ten ... all over again ...

CHAPTER 2

Great job! Let's continue with ten easy songs before we get to more difficult ones. Remember, these too will be played with your right hand

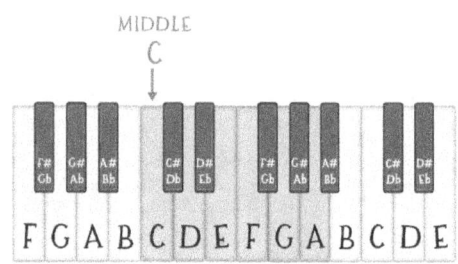

OVER IN THE MEADOW

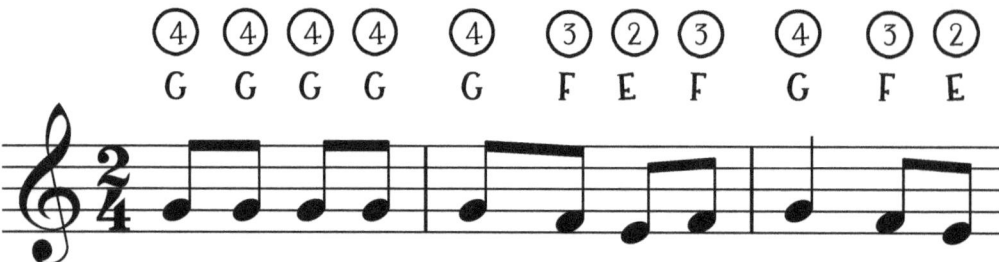

O-ver in the mea-dow in the sand in the

sun Lived an old mo-ther toa-die and her

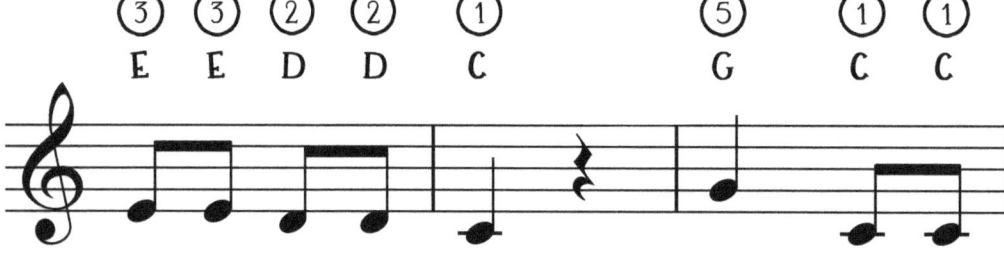

lit-tle toa-die one. "Wink," said the

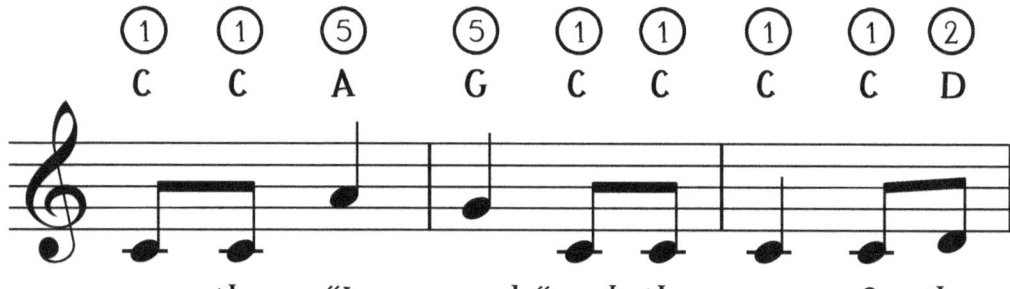

mo-ther, "I wink," said the one, So they

2

winked all day in the sand in the sun.

2. Over in the meadow, where the stream runs blue,
Lived an old mother fish and her little fishes two.
"Swim!" said the mother, "We swim!" said the two,
So they swam all day where the stream runs blue.

3. Over in the meadow in a hole in the tree,
Lived an old mother birdie and her little birdies three.
"Sing!" said the mother, "We sing!" said the three.
So they sang all day in a hole in the tree.

4. Over in the meadow in the reeds by the shore,
Lived an old mother muskrat and her little ratties four.
"Dive," said the mother, "We dive," said the four.
So they dived all day in the reeds by the shore.

5. Over in the meadow in a snug beehive,
Lived an old mother bee and her little bees five.
"Buzz," said the mother, "We buzz," said the five.
So they buzzed all day in the snug beehive.

6. Over in the meadow in a nest built of sticks,
Lived an old mother crow and her little crows six.
"Caw," said the mother, "We caw," said the six.
So they cawed all day in the nest built of sticks.

7. Over in the meadow where the grass is so even,
Lived an old mother cricket and her little crickets seven.
"Chirp!" said the mother, "We chirp!" said the seven.
So they chirped all day in the grass soft and even.

8. Over in the meadow by the old mossy gate
Lived an old mother lizard and her little lizards eight.
"Bask!" said the mother, "We bask!" said the eight.
So they basked all day on the old mossy gate.

9. Over in the meadow where they quiet pools shine
Lived a green mother frog and her little froggies nine.
"Croak!" said the mother, "We croak!" said the nine.
So they croaked all day where the quiet pools shine.

10. Over in the meadow in a sly little den
Lived an old mother spider and her little spiders ten.
"Spin!" said the mother; "We spin!" said the ten.
So they spun all day in their sly little den.

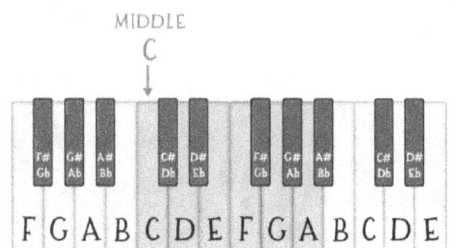

Helpful tip at the end of the song!

LAVENDER'S BLUE

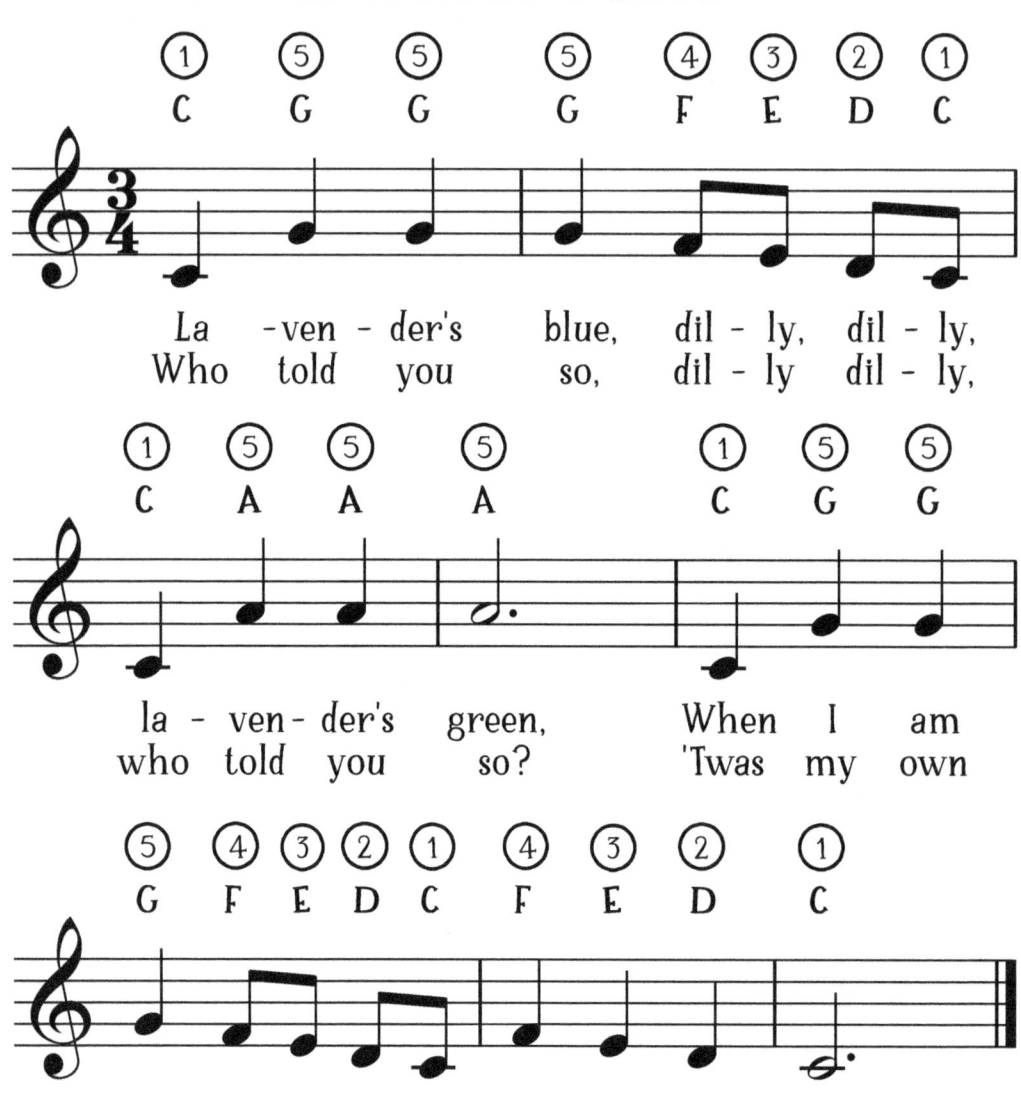

La-ven-der's blue, dil-ly, dil-ly, la-ven-der's green, When I am king, dil-ly, dil-ly, you shall be queen.
Who told you so, dil-ly dil-ly, who told you so? 'Twas my own heart, dil-ly dil-ly, that told me so.

2. Call up your men, dilly, dilly, set them to work
   Some to the plow, dilly, dilly, some to the fork,
   Some to make hay, dilly, dilly, some to cut corn,
   While you and I, dilly, dilly, keep ourselves warm.

3. Lavender's green, dilly, dilly, Lavender's blue,
   If you love me, dilly, dilly, I will love you.
   Let the birds sing, dilly, dilly, And the lambs play;
   We shall be safe, dilly, dilly, out of harm's way.

4. I love to dance, dilly, dilly, I love to sing;
   When I am queen, dilly, dilly, You'll be my king.
   Who told me so, dilly, dilly, Who told me so?
   I told myself, dilly, dilly, I told me so.

 TIP:

Notice that in this song we have a ¾ time signature. But what does this mean?

¾ in music tells us there are 3 beats in each bar. It's like counting 1-2-3 over and over. Each beat is as long as a quarter note.

Are there any notes that can last for a whole bar here? Let's think, a whole note won't work, as it's for 4/4 time. Maybe a half note? Still not quite, it's for 2/4 time. But wait!

If you look at the last bar, there's a half note with a small dot on the right. This dot is very special. It can make any note longer. So, in this case, it makes the half note last for an additional quarter note... interesting, righ?

Make sure you hold such notes for the entire bar in this song.

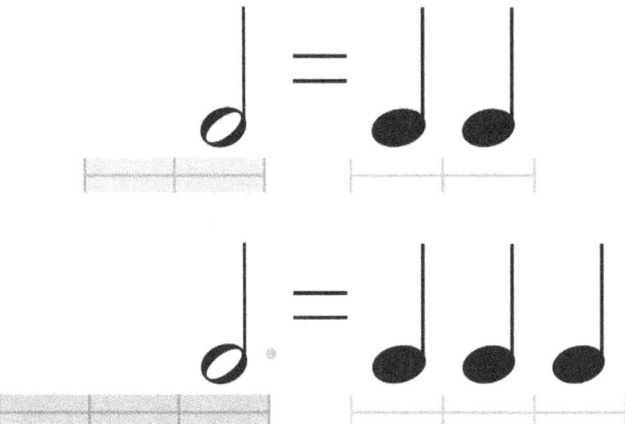

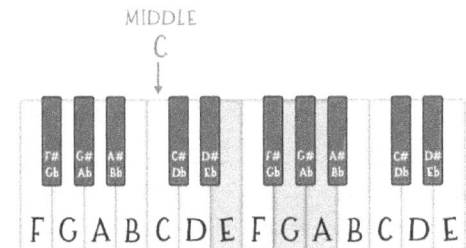

Helpful tip at
the end of
the song!

SEE-SAW MARGERY DAW

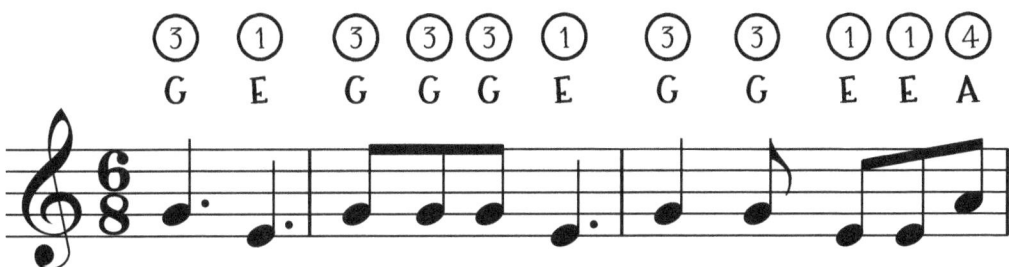

See-saw, Mar-ge-ry Daw, Jack shall have a new

mas-ter. He shall have but a pen-ny a day, Be-

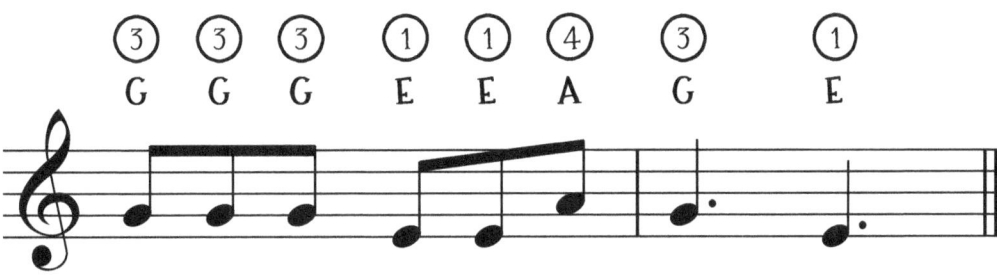

cause he won't work a - ny fas - ter.

TIP:

Pay attention to the beginning of the song, near the treble clef. We have two different numbers again! Remember that the number above tells you how many notes you can have in the bar. And the number below, what kind of notes they are.

This will help you when you play this song as well! You see number 6 above and number 8 below; this means that to play in time you need to count to six and each counting will be an eighth note.

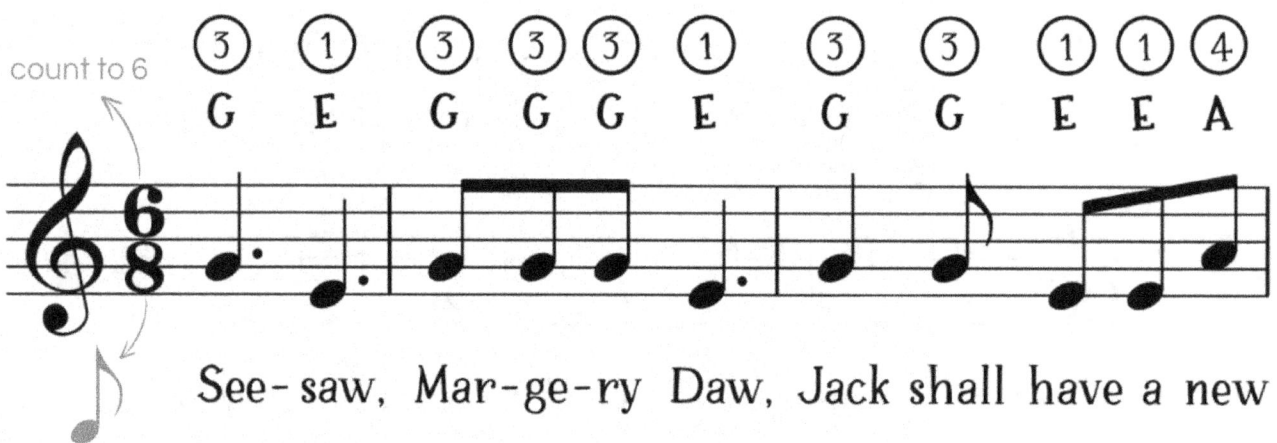

Another thing you might have noticed is that there are dots next to quarter notes. And they are working the same as with half-ones. The dot will make your quarter note longer than one eighth note.

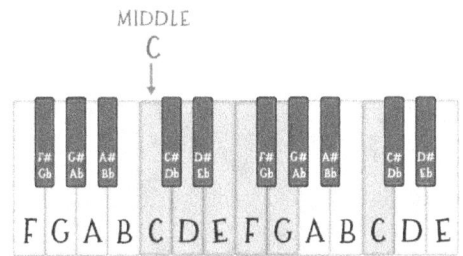

ROW, ROW, ROW YOUR BOAT

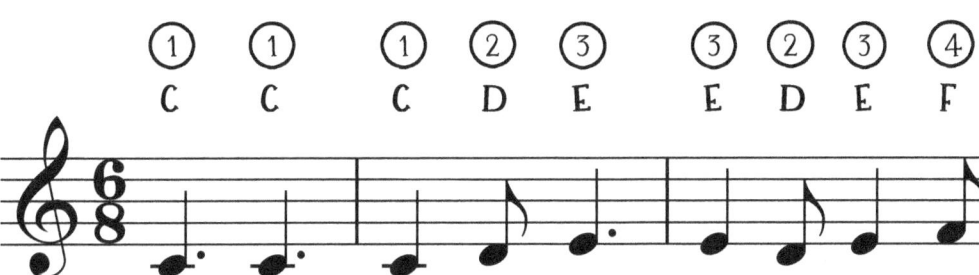

Row, row, row your boat Gent-ly down the

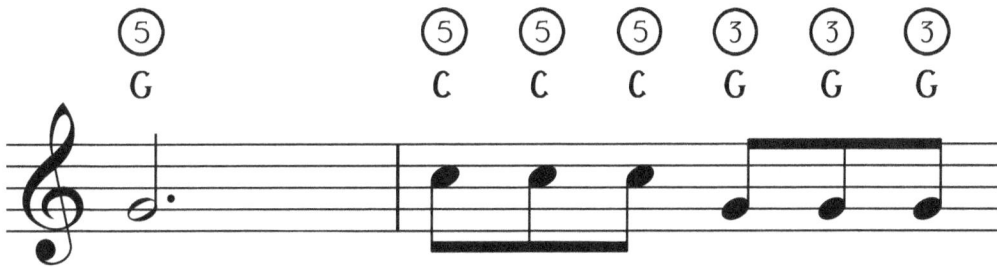

stream. Mer - ri - ly, mer - ri - ly,

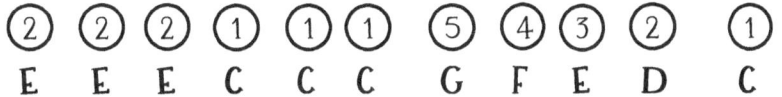

mer-ri-ly, mer-ri-ly, life is but a dream.

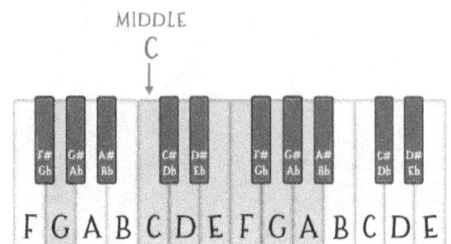

Helpful tip at the end of the song!

ARE YOU SLEEPING

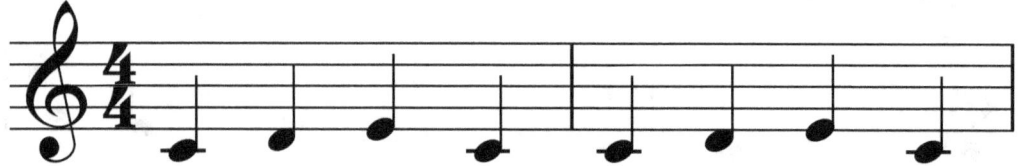

Are you sleep - ing?   Are you sleep - ing?

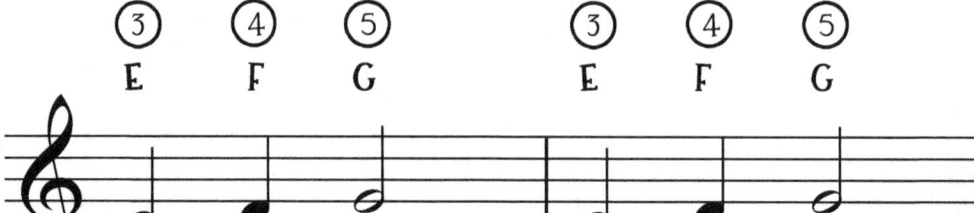

Bro - ther   John,   Bro - ther   John.

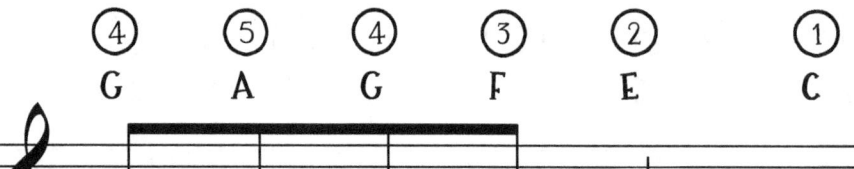

Morn - ing   bells   are   ring - ing,

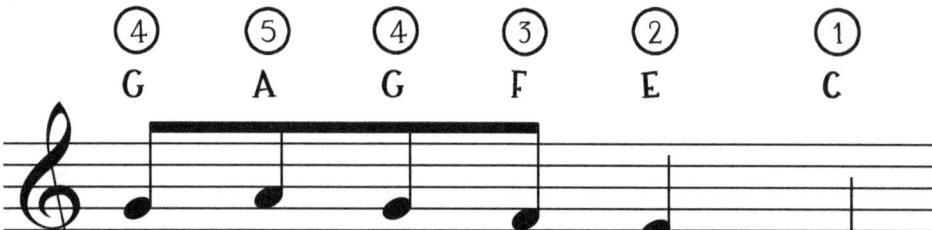

Mor - ing   bells   are   ring - ing,

TIP:

Sometimes we need lower notes, even when we have a treble clef. In this case, we will add additional lines near note heads, as if we are making the staff larger.

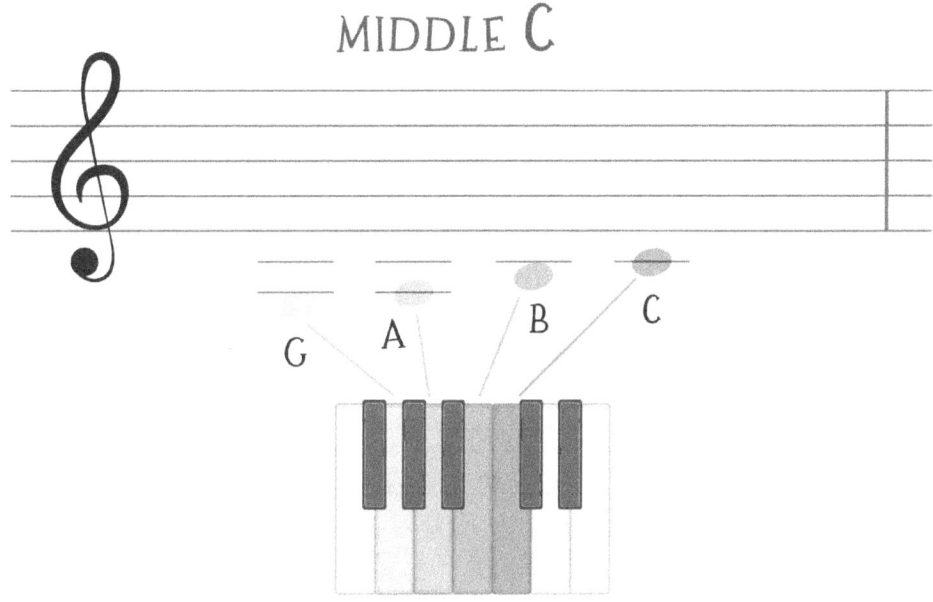

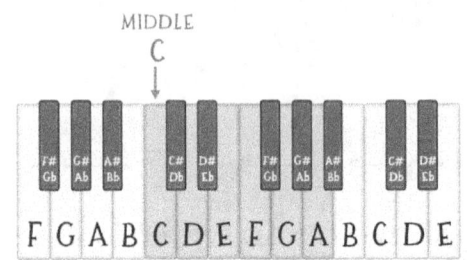

THERE'S A HOLE IN MY BUCKET

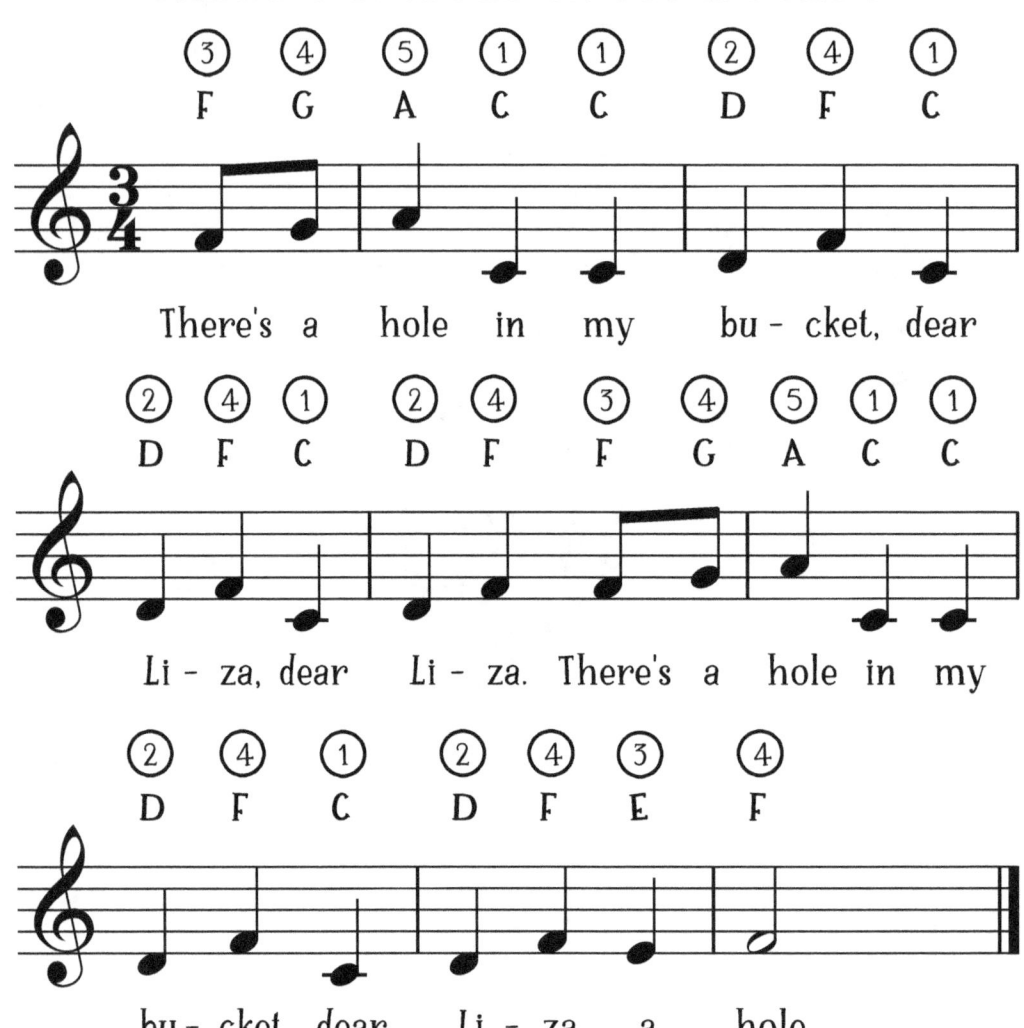

With what shall I fix it, dear Liza, dear Liza ?

The straw is too long, dear Liza, dear Liza

Then cut it, dear Henry, dear Henry, dear Henry

With what shall I cut it, dear Liza, dear Liza ?

2

With an axe, dear Henry, dear Henry, dear Henry

The axe is too dull, dear Liza, dear Liza

Then sharpen it, dear Henry, dear Henry, dear Henry

With what shall I sharpen it, dear Liza, dear Liza ?

With a stone, dear Henry, dear Henry, dear Henry

The stone is too dry, dear Liza, dear Liza

Then wet it, dear Henry, dear Henry, dear Henry

With what shall I wet it, dear Liza, dear Liza ?

With water, dear Henry, dear Henry, dear Henry

In what shall I carry it, dear Liza, dear Liza ?

In a bucket, dear Henry, dear Henry, dear Henry

There's a hole in my bucket, dear Liza, dear Liza

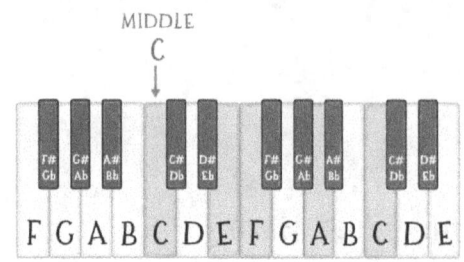

HARK, HARK! DOGS DO BARK!

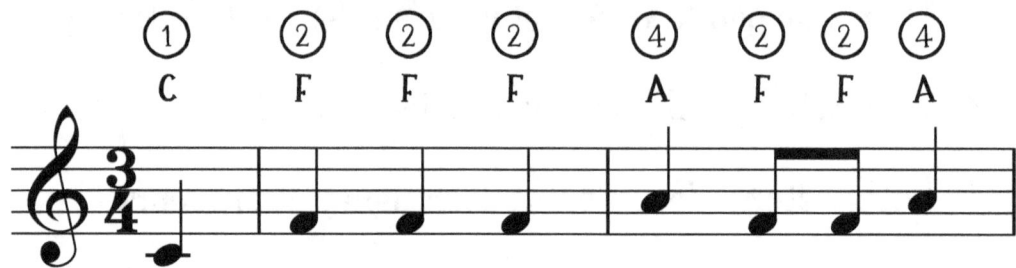

Hark, hark! Dogs do bark! Peo-ple are

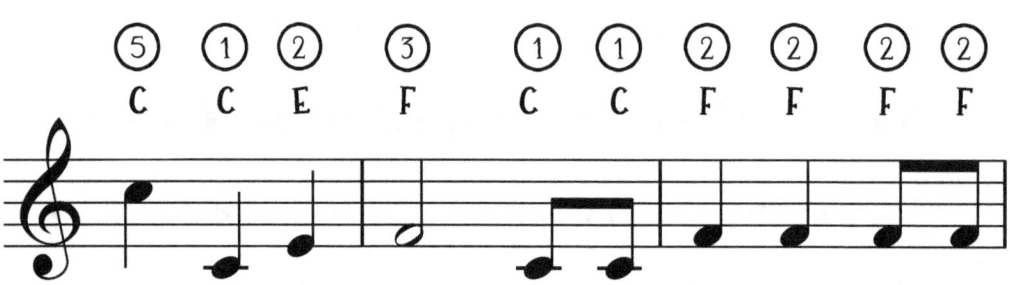

com-ing to town! Some in rags and some in

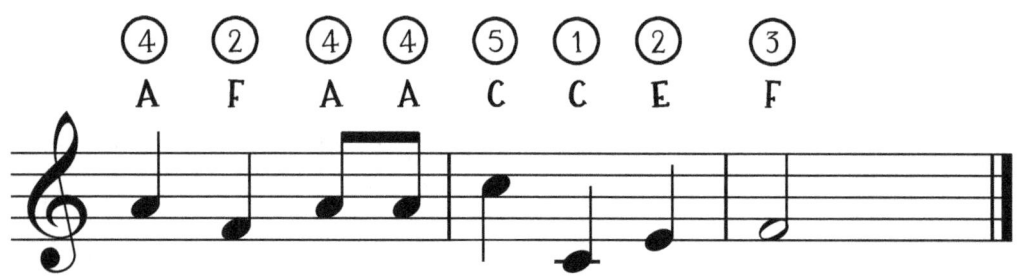

tags And some in fine vel-vet gowns.

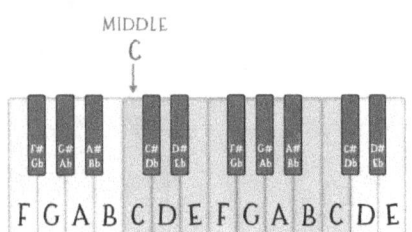

Helpful tip at the end of the song!

ST. PAUL'S STEEPLE

⑤ ④ ③ ② ① ③ ② ① ⑤
C B A G F E D C C

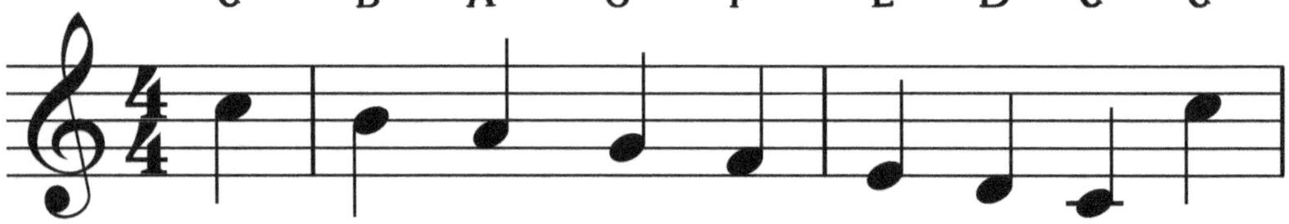

On St. Paul's stee-ple stands a tree, As

③ ② ① ⑤ ③ ② ① ⑤
A F D B G E C C

full of ap-ples as can be. The

④ ③ ② ① ③ ② ① ②
B A G F E D C E

lit-tle boys of Lon-don town, They

③ ⑤ ① ④ ⑤ ③ ② ①
F A D B C G E D

run with hooks to Pull them down. And

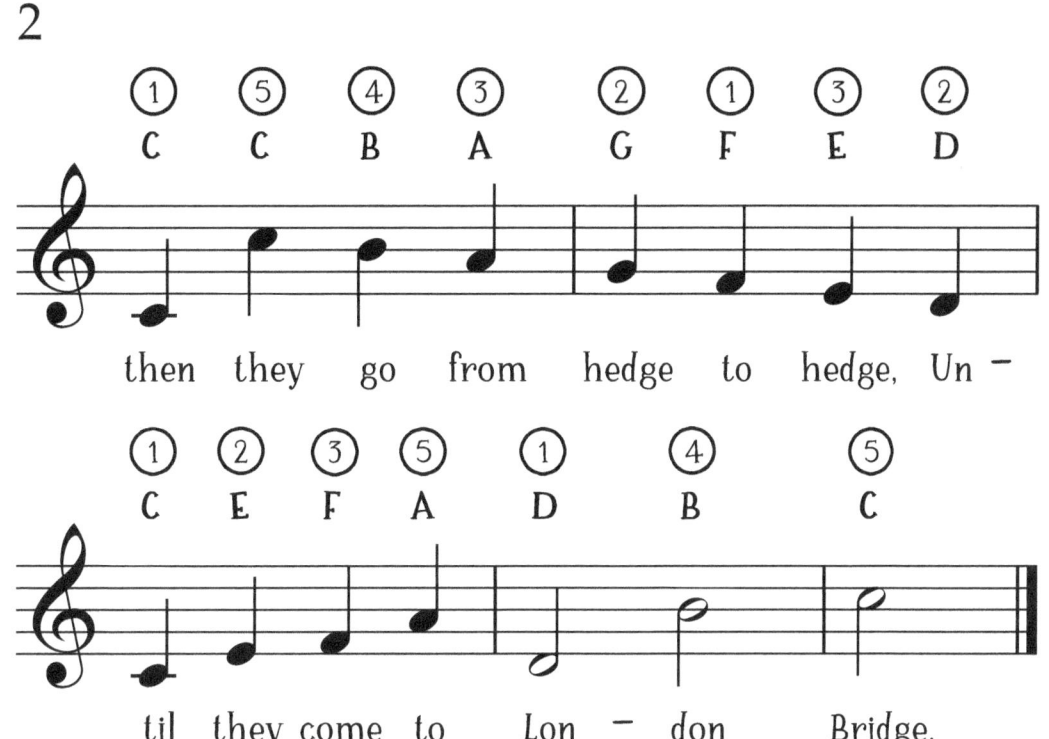

TIP

In this song, there are numerous instances where the melody descends smoothly, with notes falling one after the other without any leaps. To make it sound seamless, play it one note at a time from the fifth finger to the first.

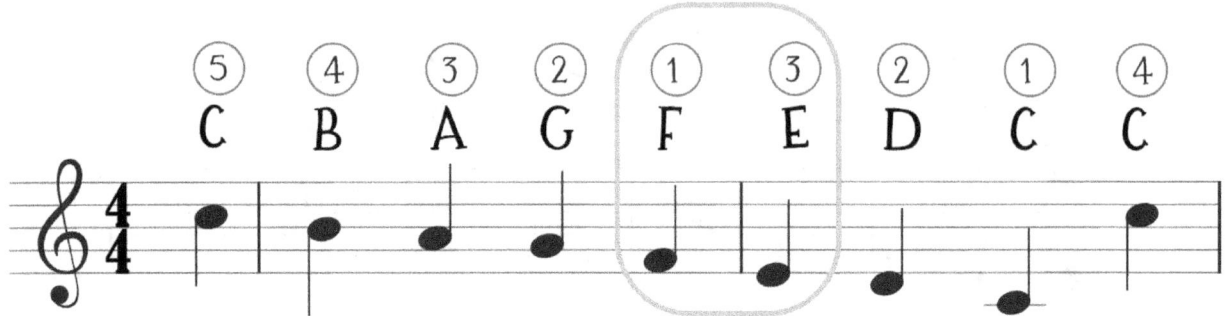

So, we need to try a new way to switch fingers. When you reach the thumb, you should keep the key pressed and slightly move your hand to the right, so the next note will be under your third finger. It's similar to closing your fingers into a fist, but not completely. (There needs to be an illustration.) When the next note is under your third finger, you can press it and release your thumb.

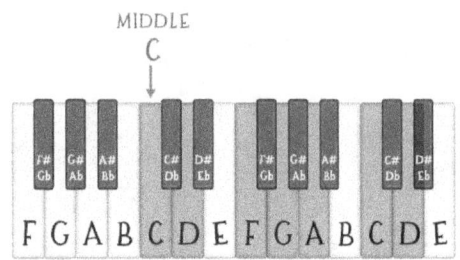

FROG WENT A-COURTING

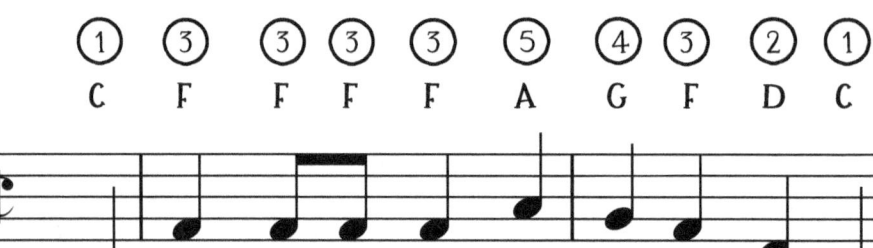

A frog went a-court-in' he did ride, a-

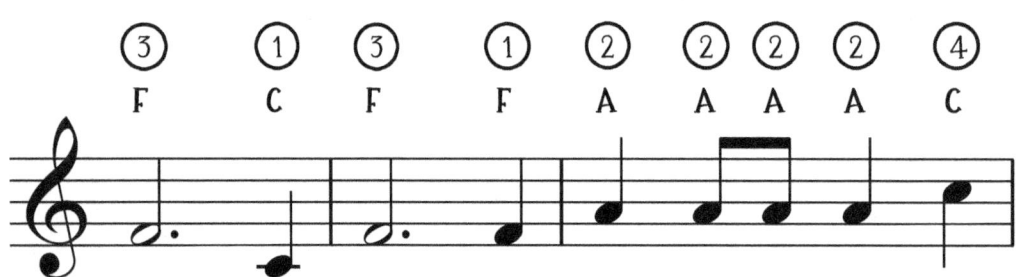

ha, ho ho. A frog went a-court-in',

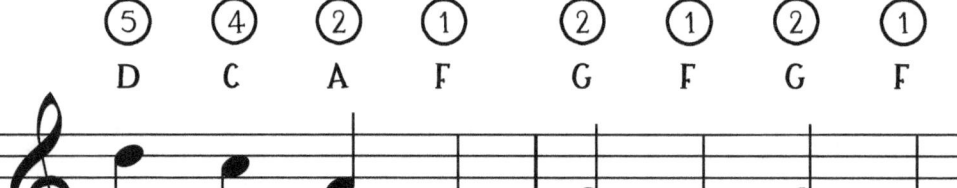

he did ride, With sword and pis-tol

by his side, a-ha, ho ho.

2

2. Well he rode down to Miss Mouse's door...
   Where he had often been before.
3. He took Miss Mousie on his knee...
   Said "Miss Mousie will you marry me..."
4. I'll have to ask my Uncle Rat
   See what he will say to that
5. Well, Uncle Rat laughed and shook his fat sides
   To think his niece would be a bride
6. Well, Uncle Rat rode off to town
   To buy his niece a wedding gown
7. Where will the wedding supper be
   Way down yonder in a hollow tree
8. What will the wedding supper be
   A fried mosquito and a roasted flea
9. First to come in were to little ants
   Fixing around to have a dance
10. Next to come in was a bumble bee
    Bouncing a fiddle on his knee
11. Next to come in was a fat sassy lad
    Thinks himself as big as his dad
12. Thinks himself a man indeed
    Because he chews the tobacco weed
13. And next to come in was a big tomcat
    He swallowed the frog and the mouse and the rat

MIDDLE
C
F# Gb
G# Ab
A# Bb
C# Db
D# Eb
F# Gb
G# Ab
A# Bb
C# Db
D# Eb
F G A B C D E F G A B C D E

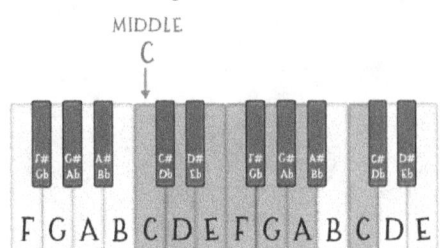

Helpful tip at the end of the song!

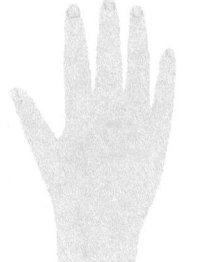

ON TOP OF OLD SMOKEY

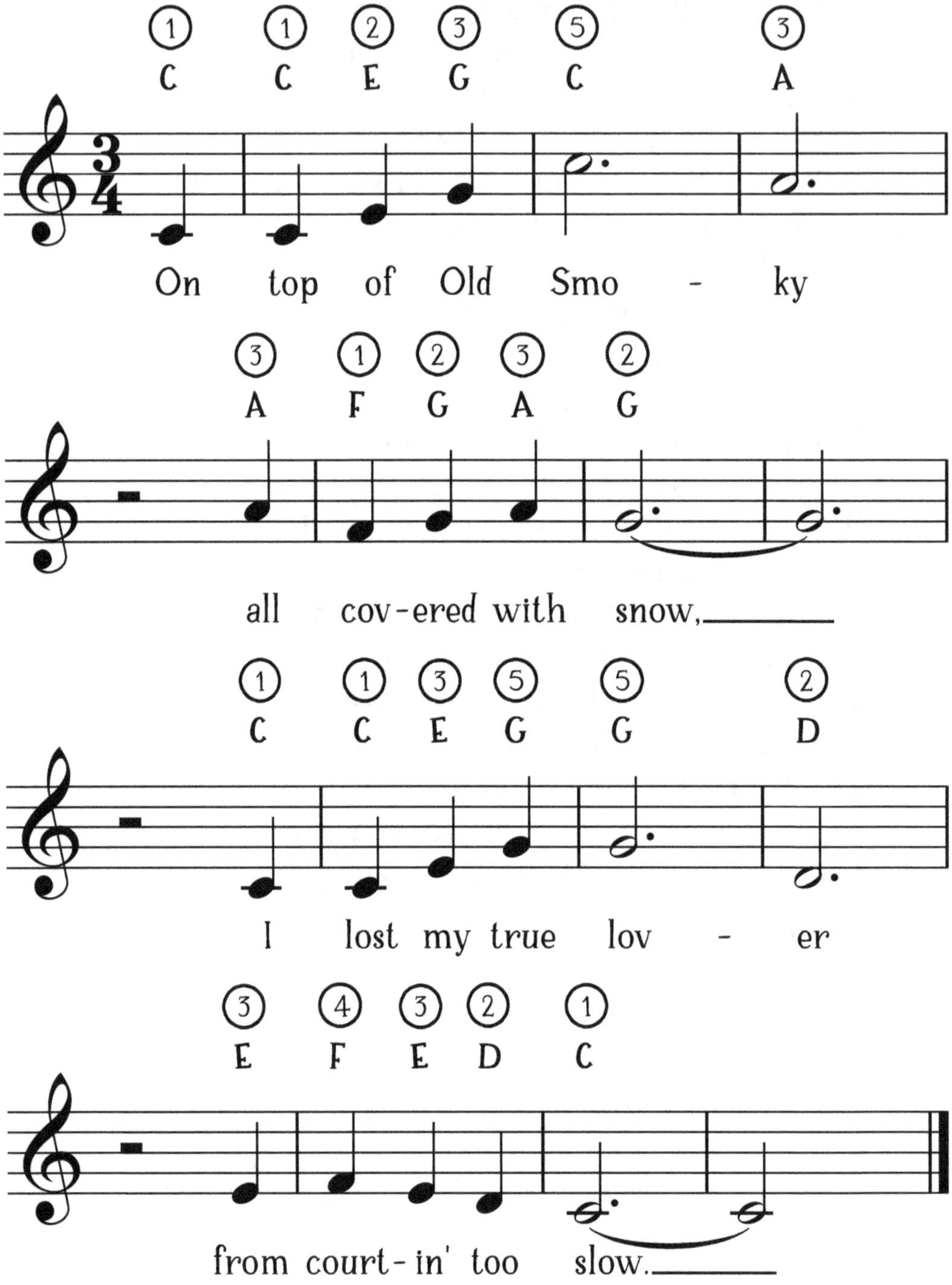

1 1 2 3 5 3
C C E G C A
On top of Old Smo - ky
3 1 2 3 2
A F G A G
all cov-ered with snow,
1 1 3 5 5 2
C C E G G D
I lost my true lov - er
3 4 3 2 1
E F E D C
from court-in' too slow.

2

2. A thief will just rob you and take what you have,
   But a false-hearted lover will lead you to the grave.

3. The grave will decay you, and turn you to dust
   Not one boy in a hundred a poor girl can trust.

4. They'll hug you and kiss you and tell you more lies,
   Than the crossties on the railroad
   or the stars in the skies.

5. For the leaves they will wither
   and the roots they will die,
   You'll all be forsaken and never know why.

6. On top of Old Smoky all covered with snow,
   I lost my true lover from courtin' too

On this fragment of the song, you see a curved line that connects two G notes. It's called a tie, and it means that you shouldn't repeat the second note. Instead, you are supposed to hold the key for the whole time these both notes last.

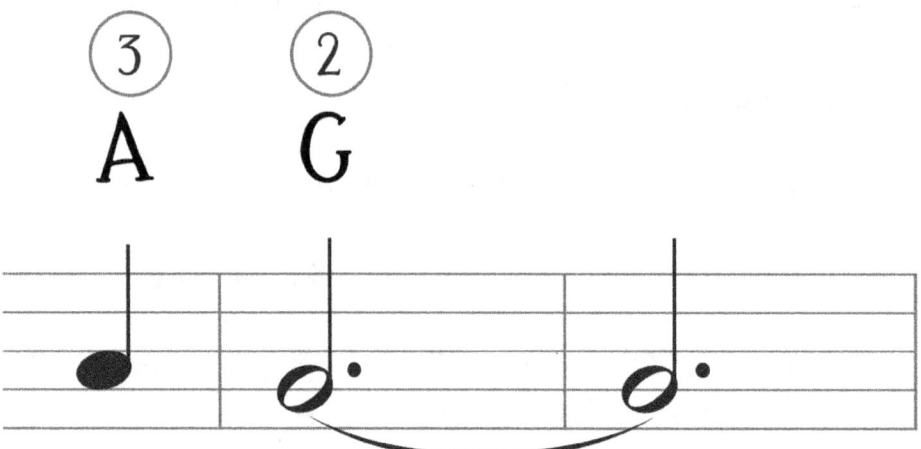

CHAPTER 3

Hey buddy! You can see now that the songs are written on two staffs. This means that now you need to play with two hands. It's very simple:

★ Use the right hand for the staff on the top
★ Use the left hand for the staff on the bottom

Pay attention to the keyboard that appears on each song, Light grey is for the right hand, dark grey for the left hand.

The rest works absolutely the same as it did before. How exciting! Now, let's play!

POLLY, WOLLY DOODLE

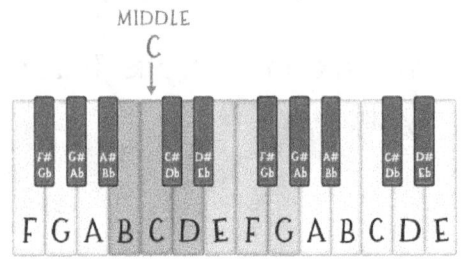

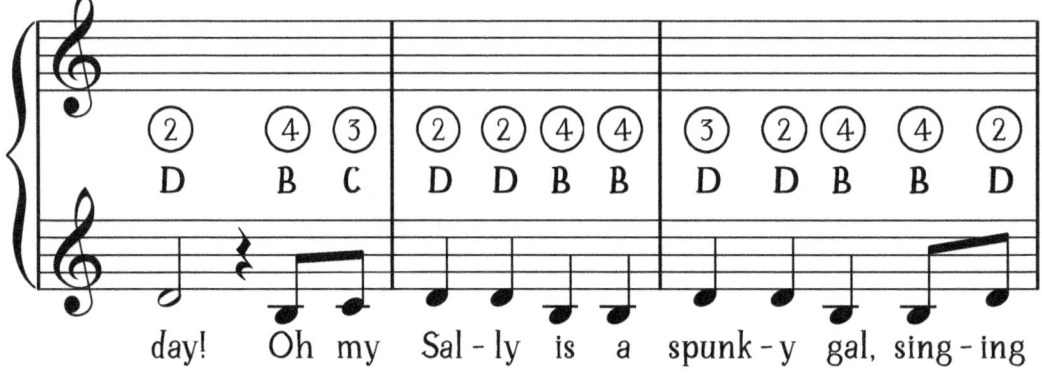

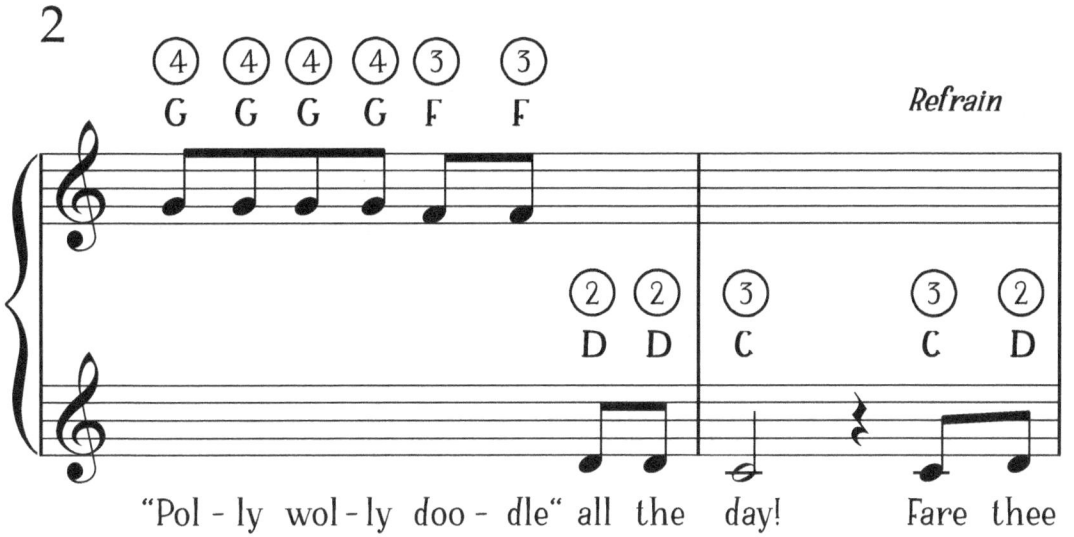
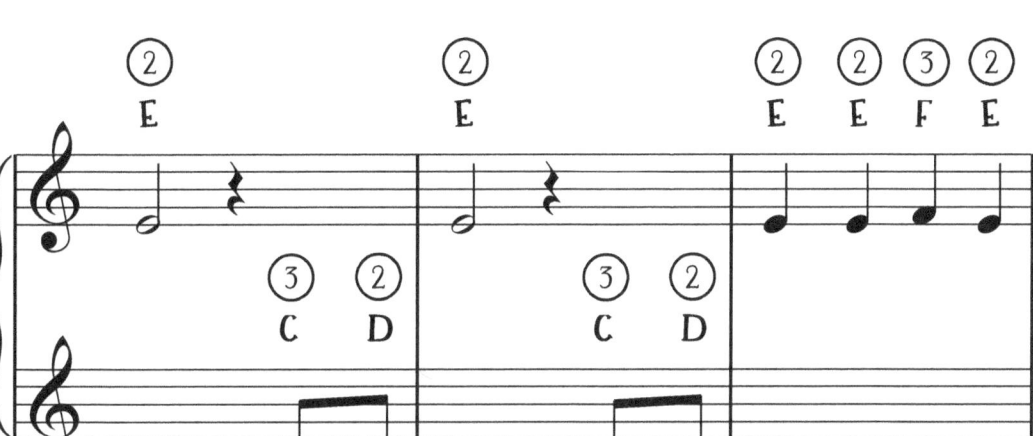

3

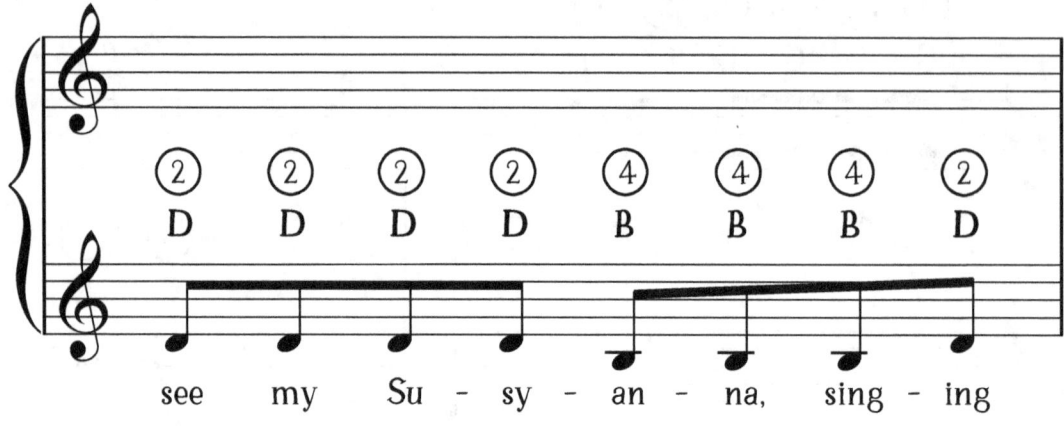

see my Su - sy - an - na, sing - ing

"Pol - ly wol - ly doo - dle" all the day!

2. Oh, my Sal, she is
   A maiden fair
   Sing Polly wolly doodle
   all the day
   With curly eyes
   And laughing hair
   Sing Polly wolly doodle
   all the day

   Refrain

3. Behind the barn,
   Down on my knees
   Sing Polly wolly doodle
   all the day
   I thought I heard
   A chicken sneeze
   Sing Polly wolly doodle
   all the day

   Refrain

4

4. He sneezed so hard
   With the whooping cough
   Sing Polly wolly doodle
   all the day
   He sneezed his head
   And the tail right off
   Sing Polly wolly doodle
   all the day

Refrain

5. Oh, a grasshopper sittin'
   On a railroad track
   Sing Polly wolly doodle
   all the day
   A-pickin' his teeth
   With a carpet tack
   Sing Polly wolly doodle
   all the day

Refrain

6. Oh, I went to bed
   But it wasn't any use
   Sing Polly wolly doodle
   all the day
   My feet stuck out
   Like a chicken roost
   Sing Polly wolly doodle
   all the day

Refrain

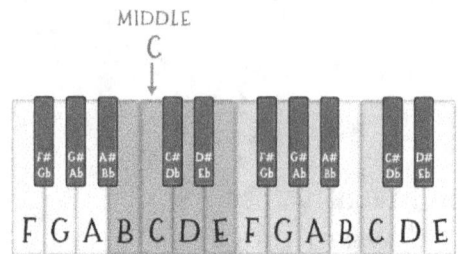

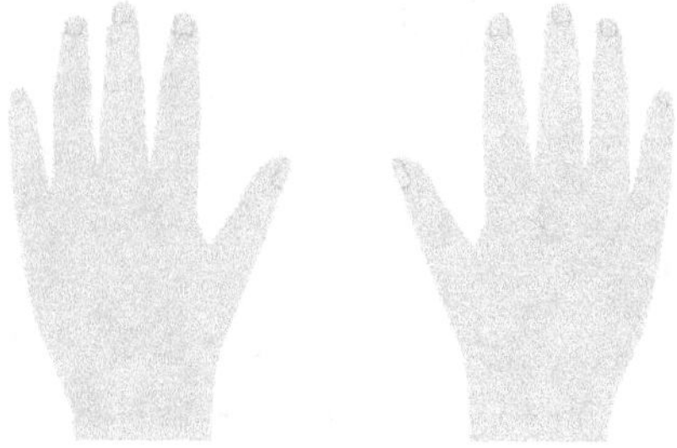

I HAD A LITTLE NUT TREE

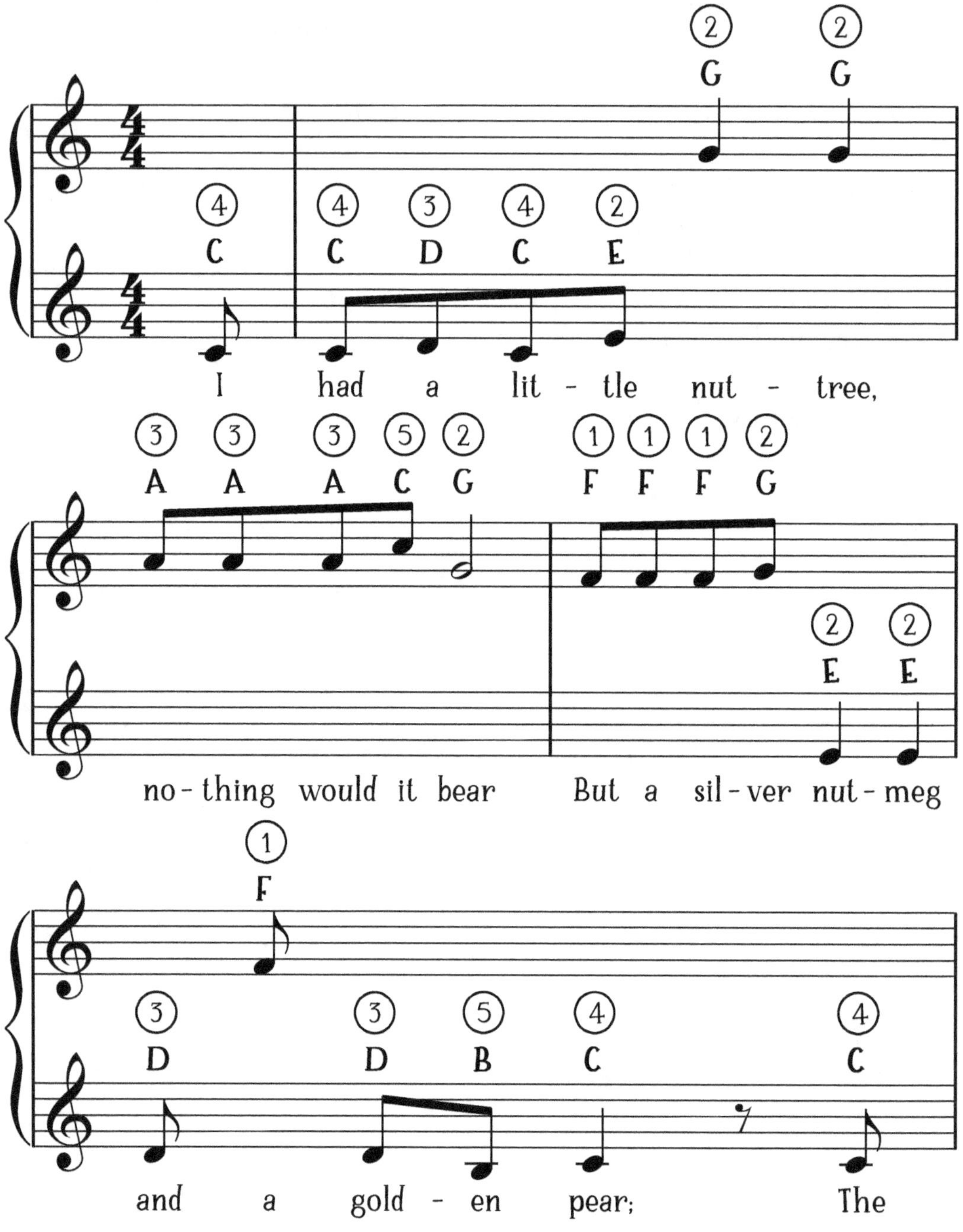

2. Her dress was made of crimson,
   Jet black was her hair,
   She asked me for my nutmeg
   And my golden pear.

3. I said, "So fair a princess
   Never did I see,
   I'll give you all the fruit
   From my little nut tree."

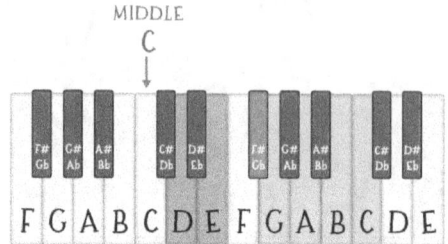

Helpful tip at the end of the song!

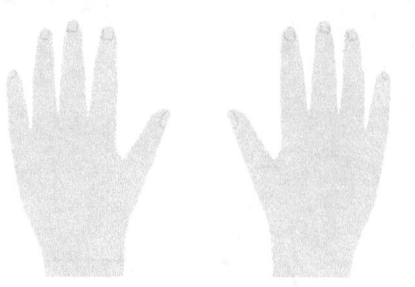

BINGO

There was a far-mer had a dog, and Bin-go was his name-o. B-I-N-G-O, B-I-N-G-O, B-I-

2

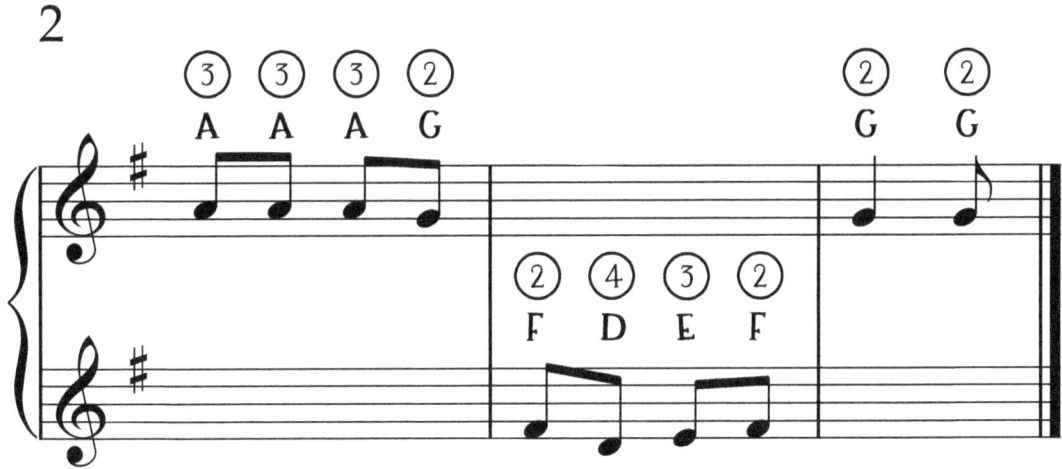

N - G - O, and Bin-go was his name - o.

2. ... (clap) - I - N - G - O, (clap) - I - N - G - O,
   (clap) - I - N - G - O, and Bingo was his name-o.

3. ... (clap) - (clap) - N - G - O,
   (clap) - (clap) - N - G - O, (clap) - (clap) - N - G - O,
   and Bingo was his name-o.

4. ... (clap) - (clap) - (clap) - G - O,
   (clap) - (clap) - (clap) - G - O,
   (clap) - (clap) - (clap) - G - O,
   and Bingo was his name-o.

5. ... (clap) - (clap) - (clap) - (clap) - O,
   (clap) - (clap) - (clap) - (clap) - O,
   (clap) - (clap) - (clap) - (clap) - O,
   and Bingo was his name-o.

6. ... (clap) - (clap) - (clap) - (clap) - (clap),
   (clap) - (clap) - (clap) - (clap) - (clap),
   (clap) - (clap) - (clap) - (clap) - (clap),
   and Bingo was his name-o.

We see a new thing here... or maybe you can recognize it. Look at the symbol next to the treble clef, at the beginning of each line. This is a sharp! Since it's placed on the last line, it's an F-sharp. You may be wondering why it's not near the notes... Well, this is because in this song, each time you see F, you should play the black key for F-sharp. You don't need to play the white F key at all. It doesn't matter where the F notes are in the song—they're all F-sharp when you see that sharp symbol near the clef.

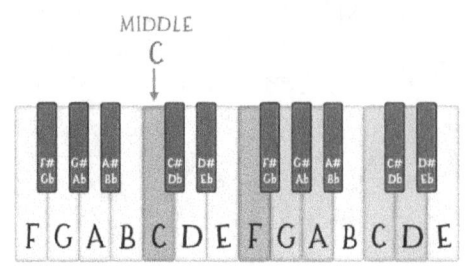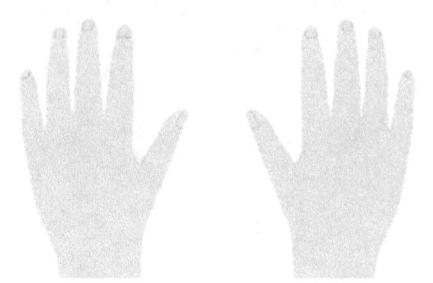

FARMER IN THE DELL

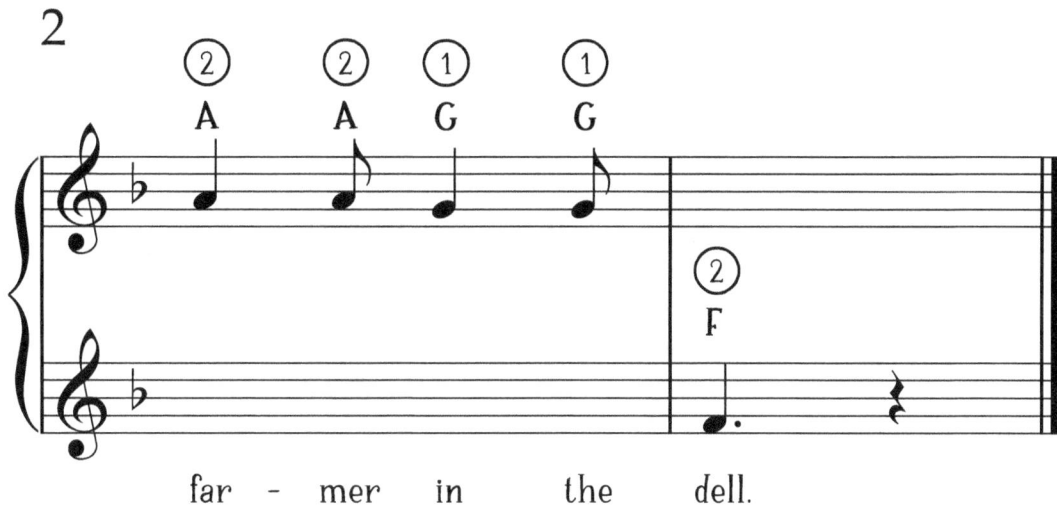

2. The farmer takes the wife...
3. The wife takes the child...
4. The child takes the nurse...
5. The nurse takes the dog...
6. The dog takes the cat...
7. The cat takes the rat....
8. The rat takes the cheese...
9. The cheese stands alone...

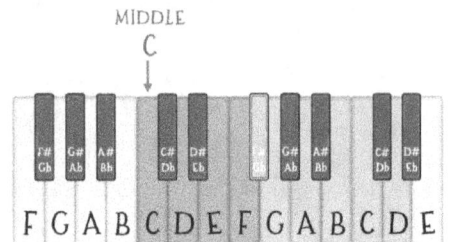
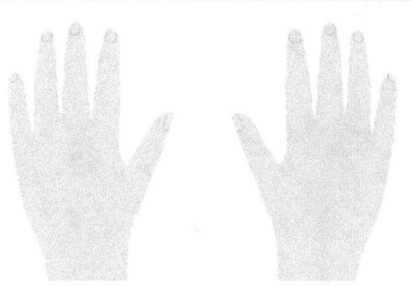

Helpful tip at the end of the song!

HEAD, SHOULDERS, KNEES AND TOES

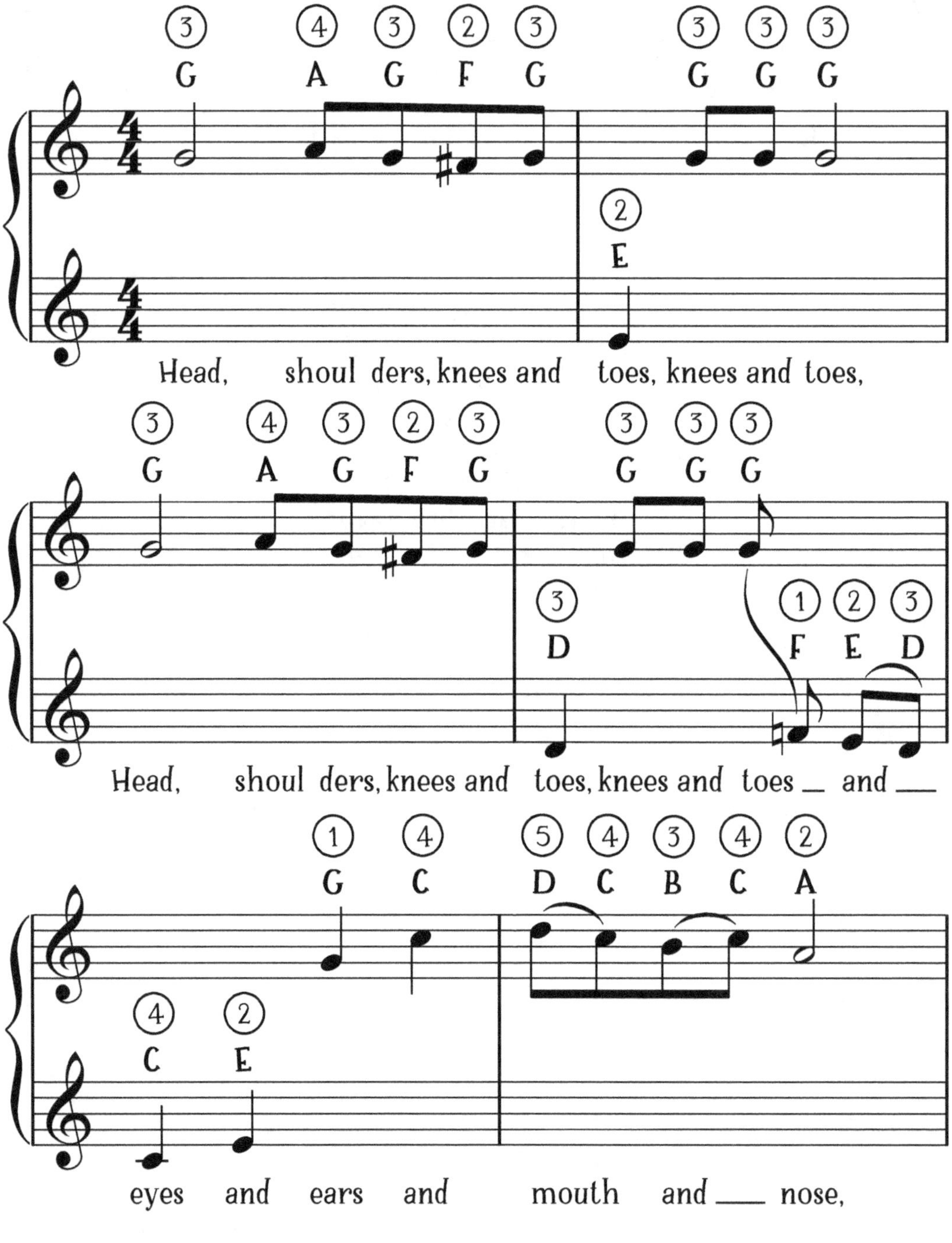

Head, shoul ders knees and toes, knees and toes.

TIP

In this song, you'll see F-sharp notes too, but not always. When you do, it will have a sharp symbol ♯ next to it, showing it should be played on the black key that is jus above the white F key.

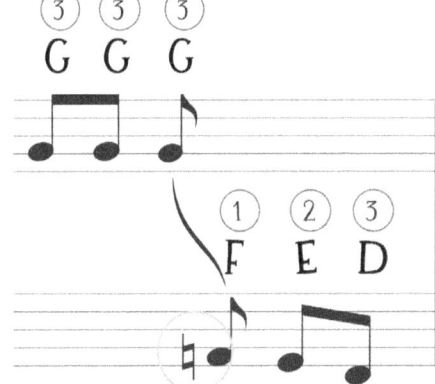

If you see a regular F note, without any sharp (or flat) symbol next to it, play the white key.

This time, you'll find the sharp next to the notes that should be played as F-sharp and not near the treble clef, as you've seen on the previous song.

MIDDLE
C
F# Gb
G# Ab
A# Bb
C# Db
D# Eb
F# Gb
G# Ab
A# Bb
C# Db
D# Eb
F G A B C D E F G A B C D E

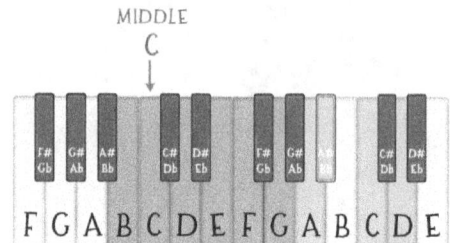

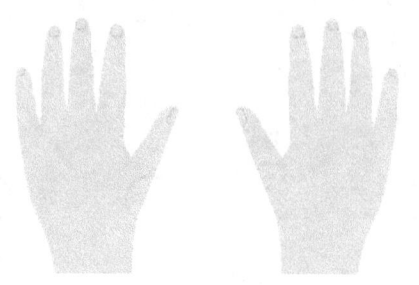

Helpful tip at the end of the song!

POLLY, PUT THE KETTLE ON

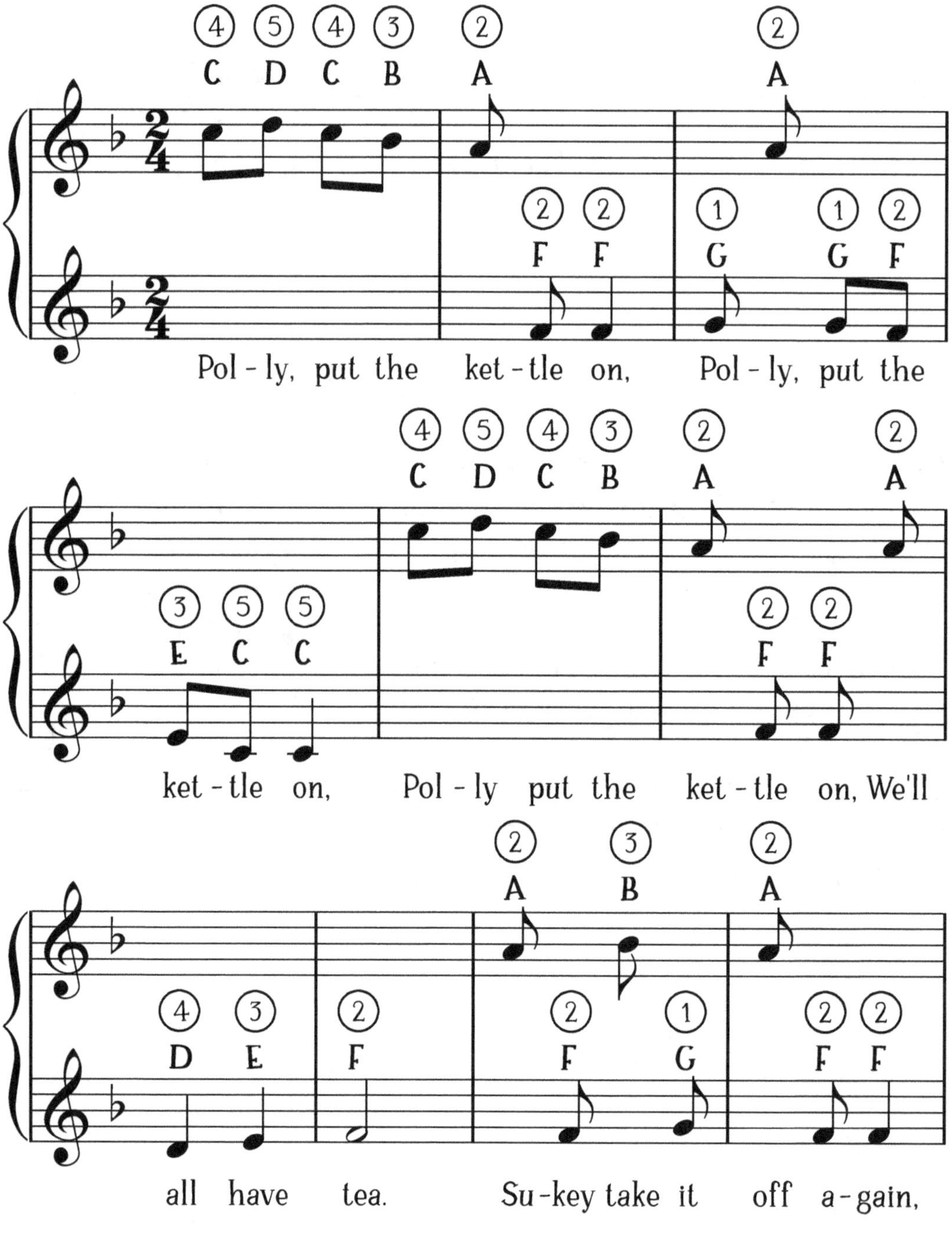

4 5 4 3 2 2
C D C B A A
2 2 1 1 2
F F G G F
Pol - ly, put the ket - tle on, Pol - ly, put the
4 5 4 3 2 2
C D C B A A
3 5 5 2 2
E C C F F
ket - tle on, Pol - ly put the ket - tle on, We'll
2 3 2
A B A
4 3 2 2 1 2 2
D E F F G F F
all have tea. Su - key take it off a - gain,

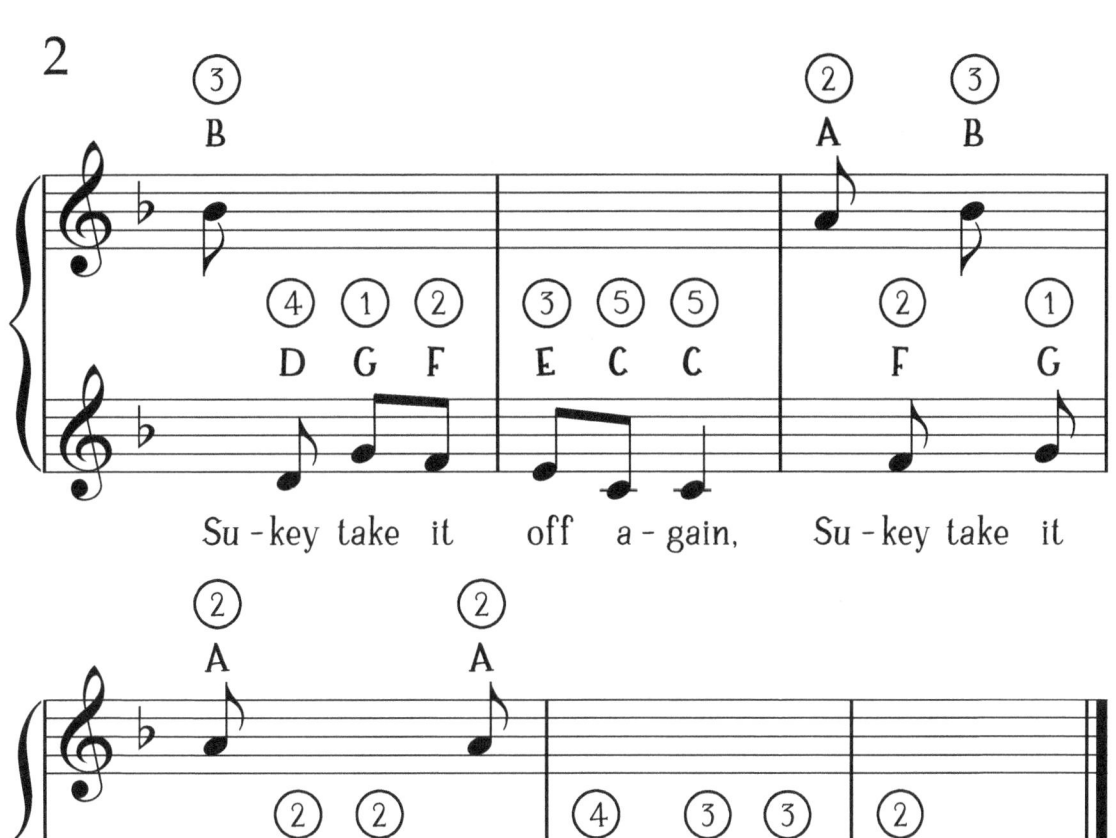

Remember you've seen F-sharp near the treble clef? Well, this time we see a flat symbol (♭) on the third line where B notes live. Whenever you see a B note with a flat symbol next to it, play the black key B-flat.

This key is called B-flat. It doesn't matter where the B notes are in the song—they're always B-flat when you see that flat symbol.

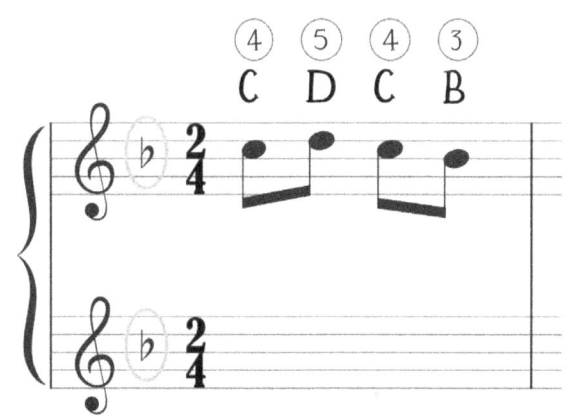

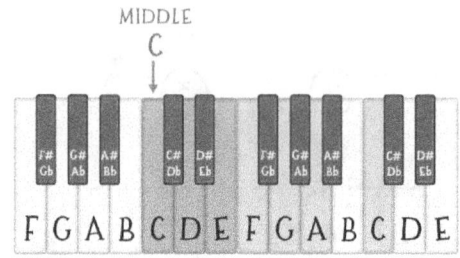

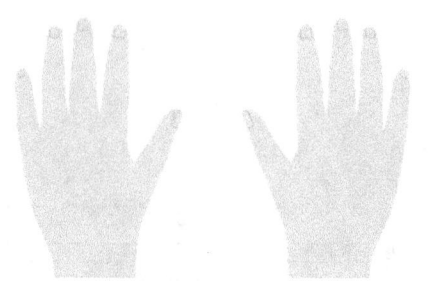

MIDDLE
C
F# Gb G# Ab A# Bb C# Db D# Eb F# Gb G# Ab A# Bb C# Db D# Eb
F G A B C D E F G A B C D E

MULBERRY BUSH

1 1 1 1 3 5 5 3 1 1
F F F F A C C A F F
Here we go 'round the mul - ber - ry bush, the
2 2 2 2 1
G G G G F
2 2 3 4
E E D C
mul - ber - ry bush, the mul - ber - ry bush.
1 1 1 1 3 5 5 3 1 1
F F F F A C C A F F
Here we go 'round the mul - ber - ry bush so

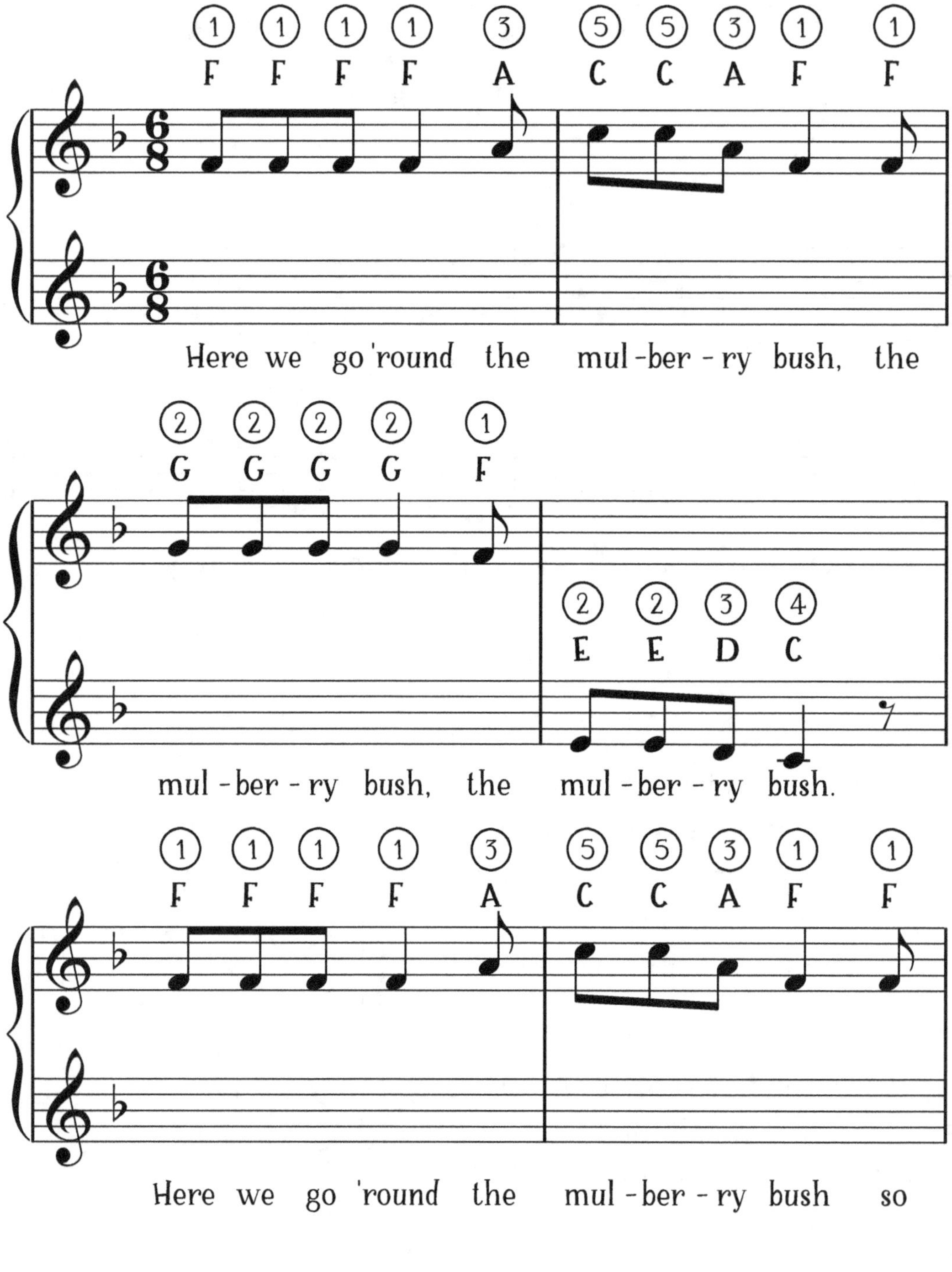

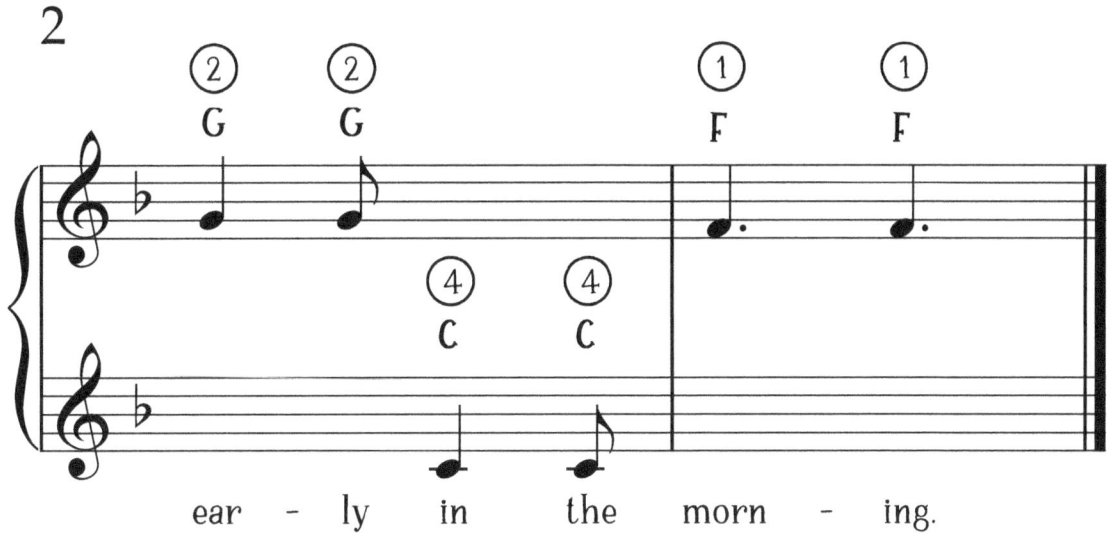

2. This is the way we wash our face,
   wash our face, wash our face.
   This is the way we wash our face,
   wash our face, wash our face,
   early in the morning.

3. This is the way we comb our hair...

4. This is the way we brush our teeth...

5. This is the way we put on our clothes...

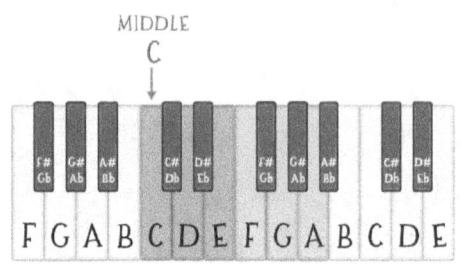

HICKORY DICKORY DOCK

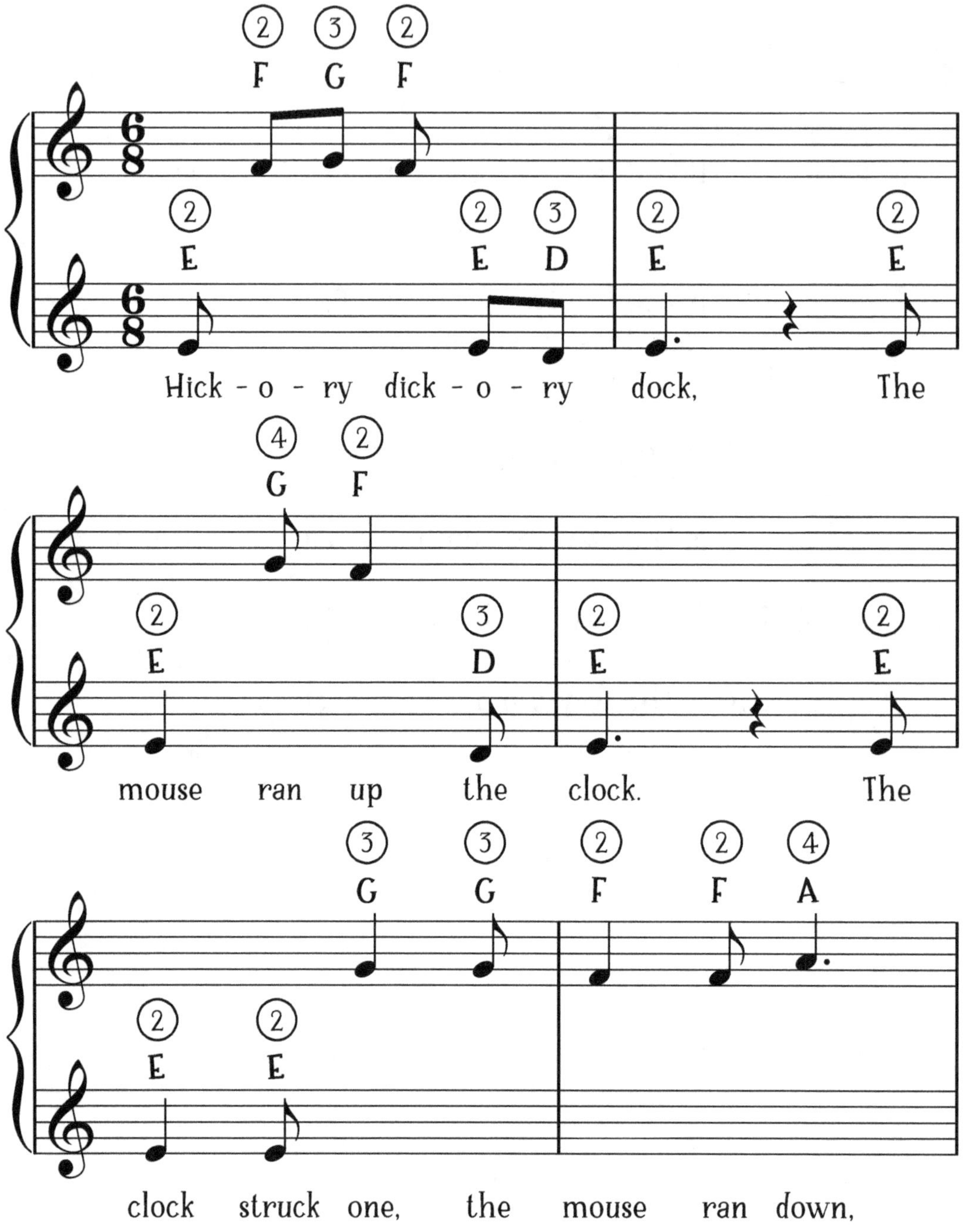

Hick - o - ry dick - o - ry dock, The mouse ran up the clock. The clock struck one, the mouse ran down,

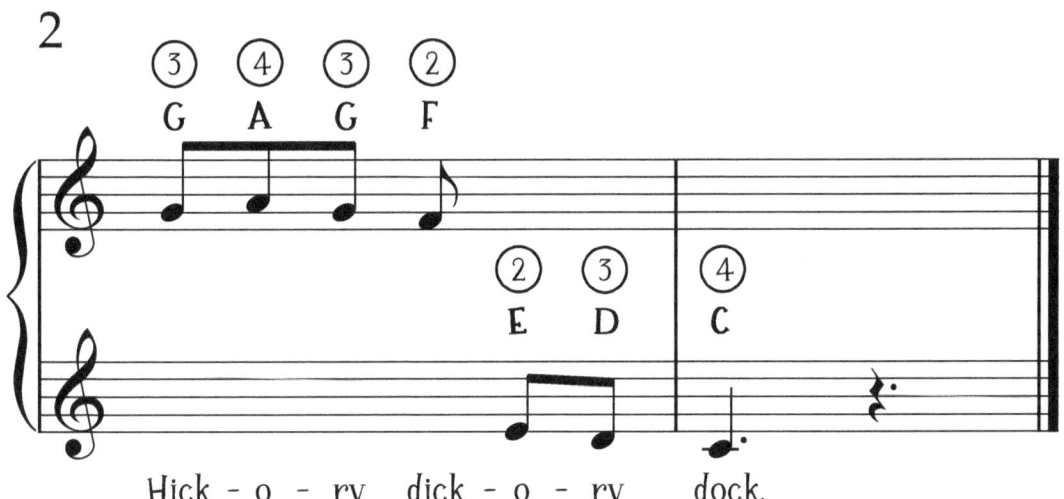

2. ... two... 3. ... three... 4. ... four... 5. ... five... 6. ...six...
7. ... seven... 8. ...eight... 9. ... nine... 10. ... ten... .

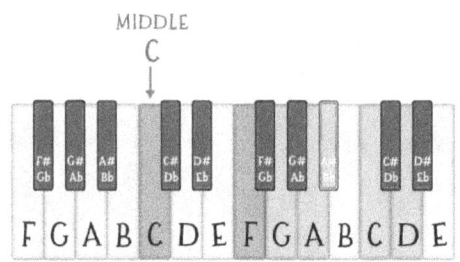

POP GOES THE WEASEL

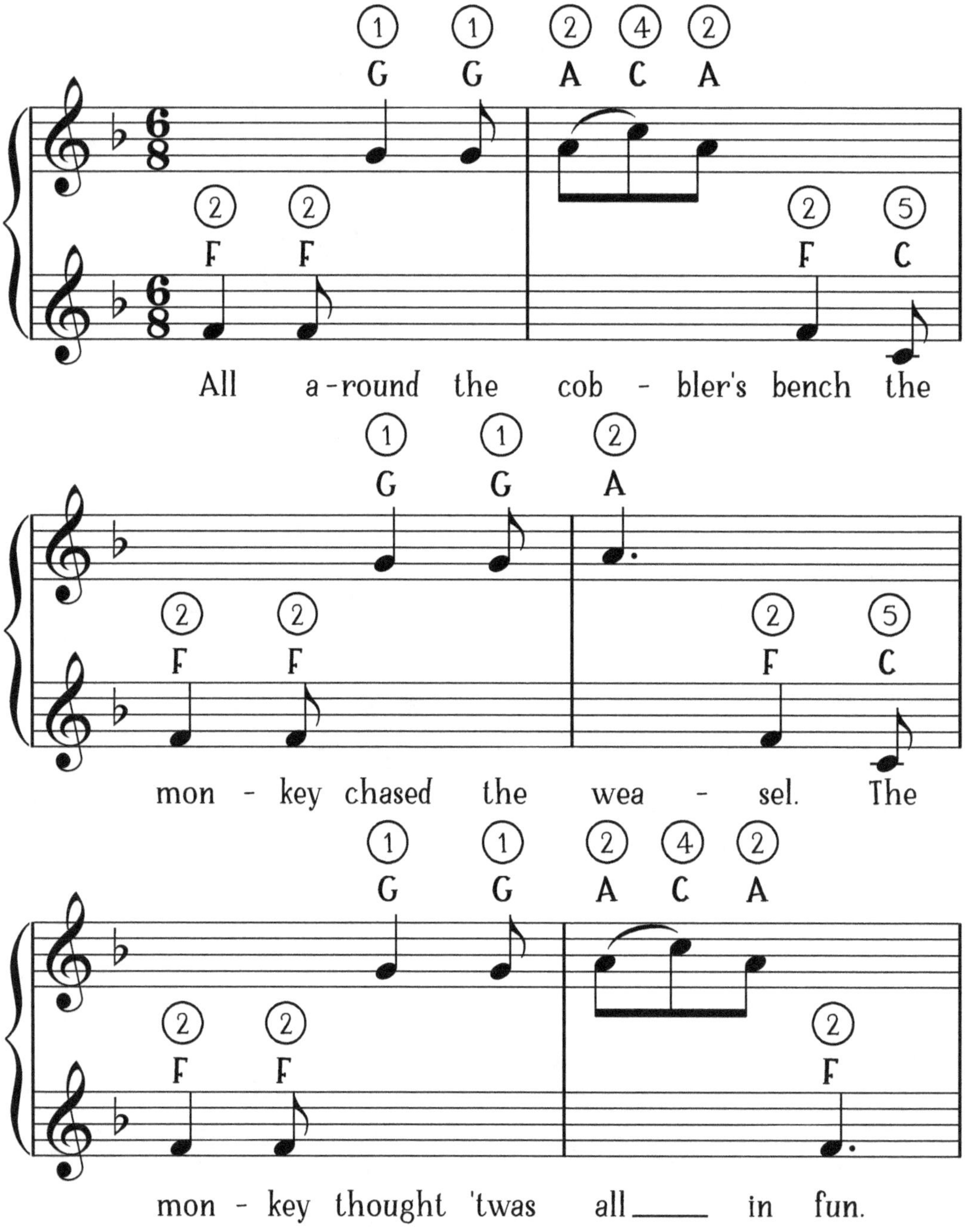

2

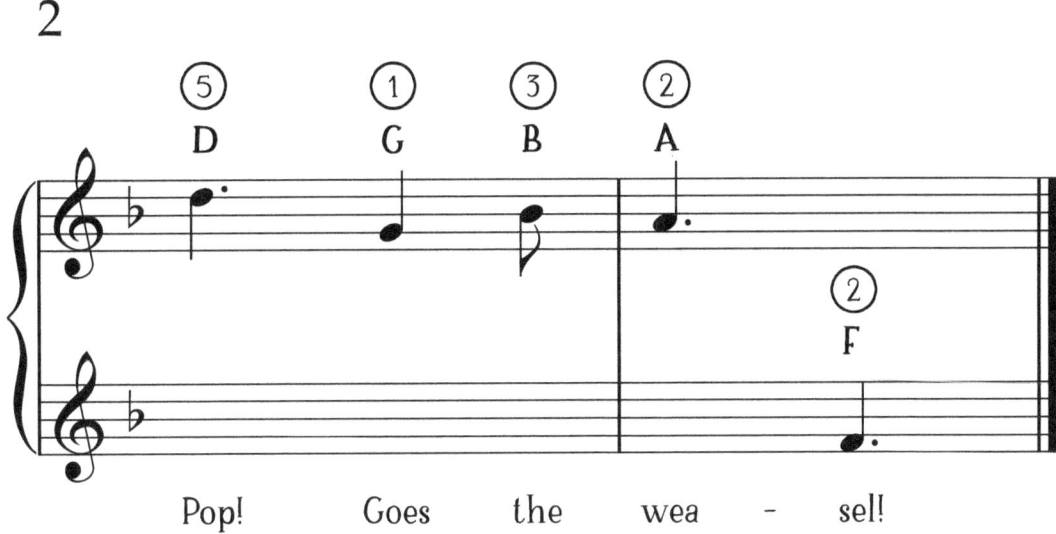

Pop! Goes the wea - sel!

2. Johnny's got the whooping cough and
   Mary's got the measles
   That's the way the money goes.
   Pop! Goes the weasel!

3. A penny for a spool of thread
   A penny for a needle,
   That's the way the money goes.
   Pop! Goes the weasel!

4. I've no time to plead and pine,
   I've no time to wheedle,
   Kiss me quick and then I'm gone.
   Pop! Goes the weasel!

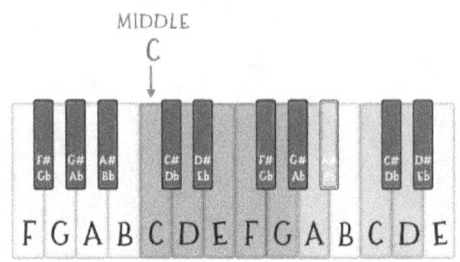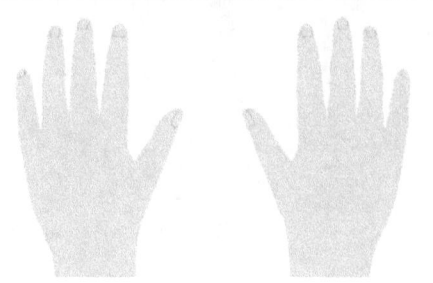

HEY DIDDLE DIDDLE

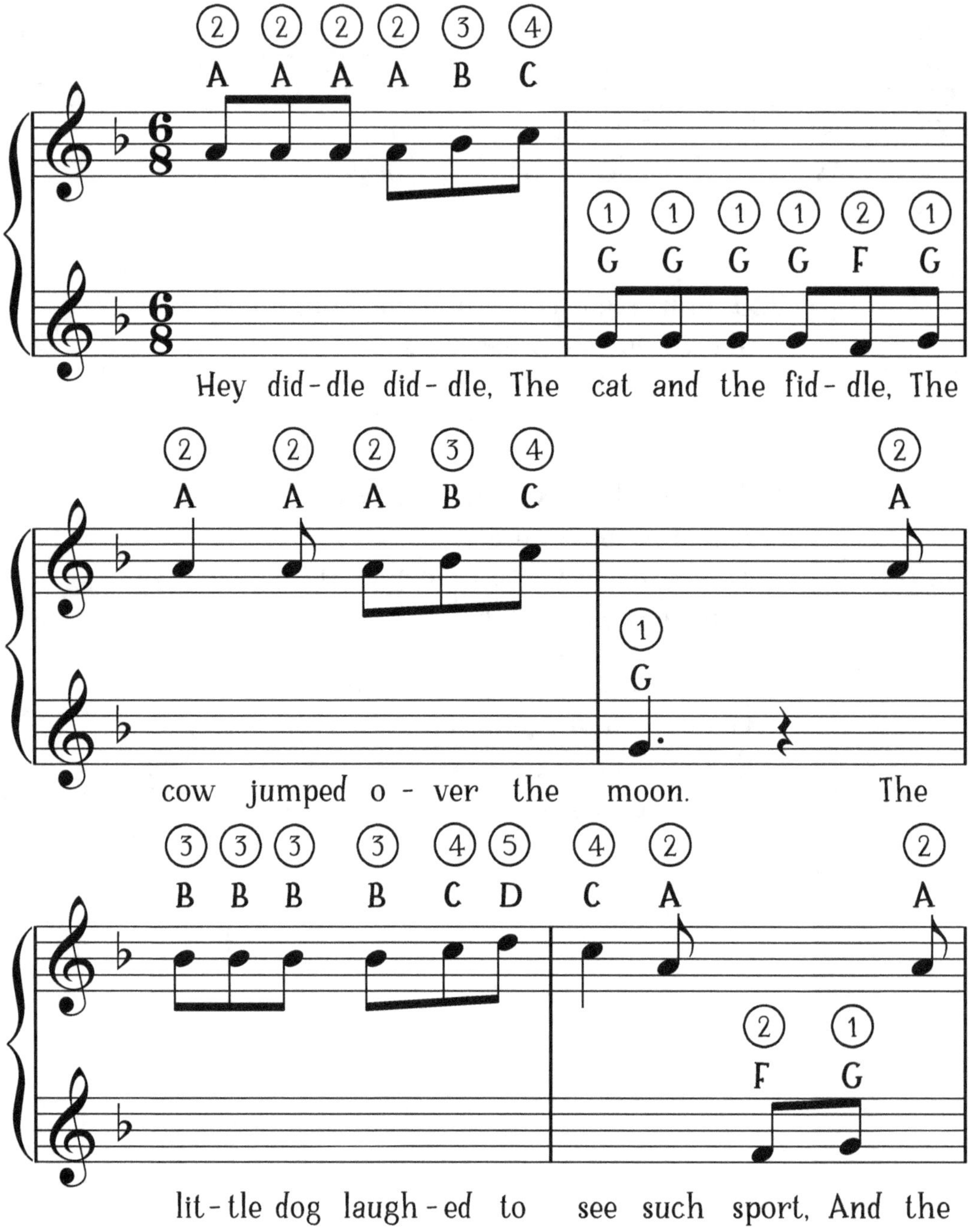

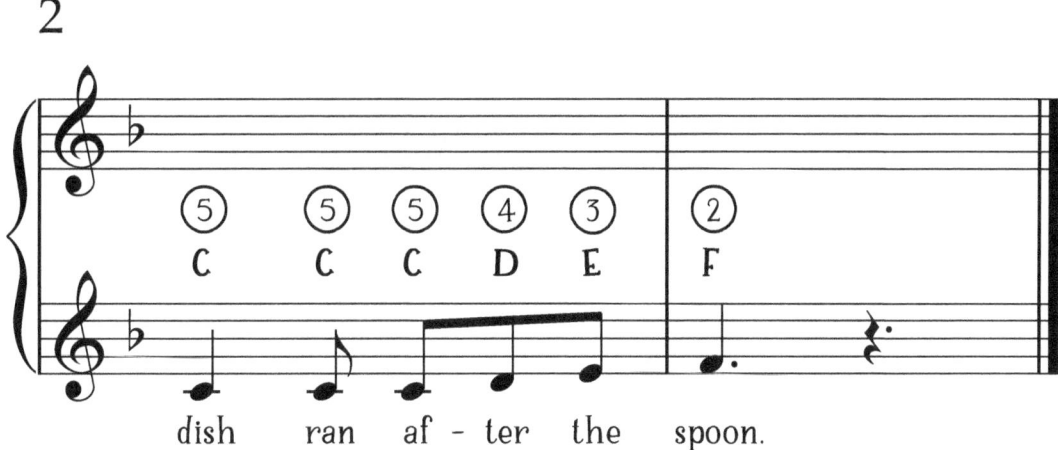

CHAPTER 4

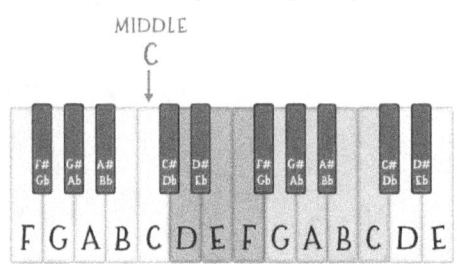

RIG-A-JIG-JIG

② ② ② ② ② ③ ②
G G G G G A G

③
E

As I was walk-ing down the street,

② ③ ② ②
G   A G G

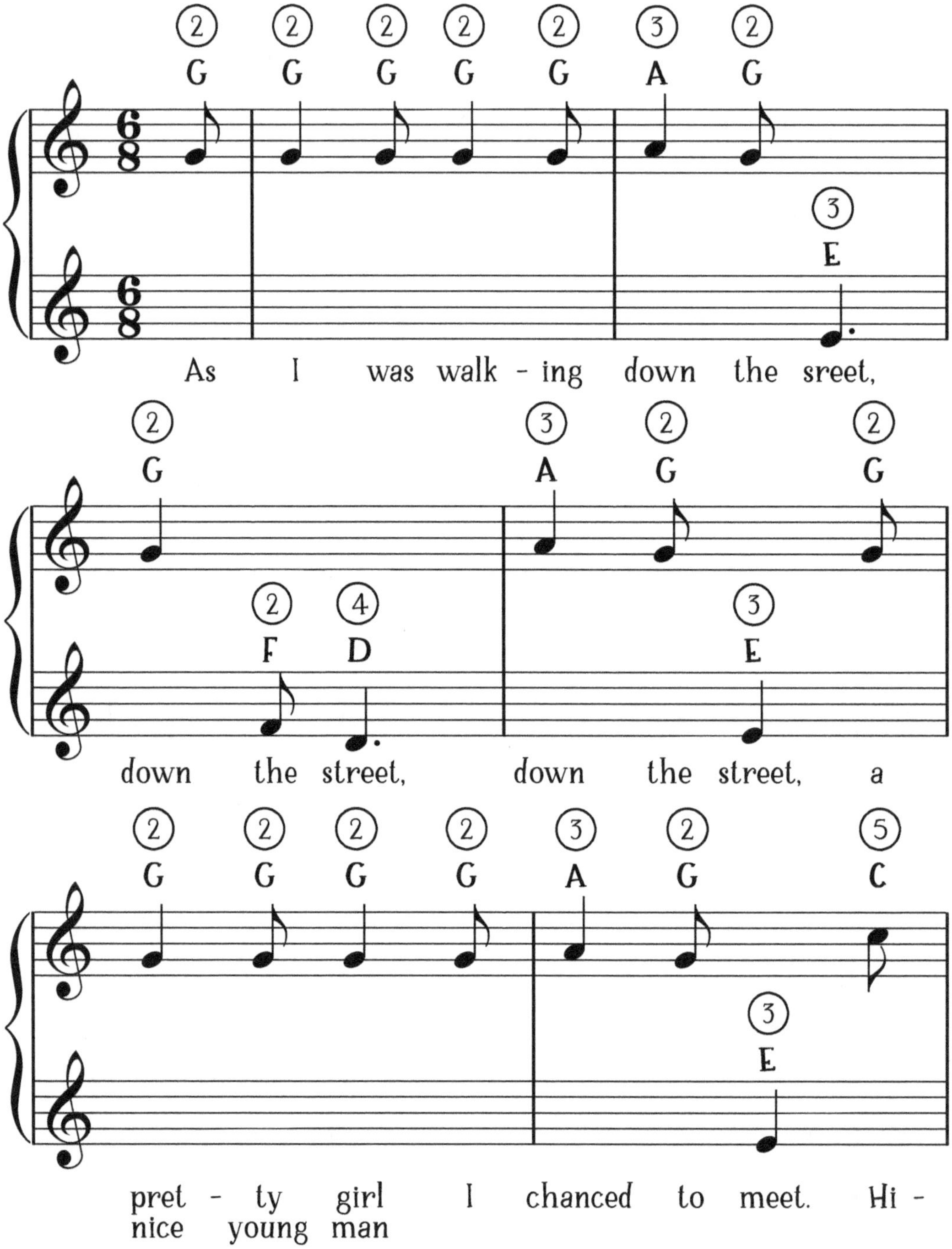

② ④   ③
F D   E

down the street, down the street, a

② ② ② ② ③ ② ⑤
G G G G A G C

③
E

pret - ty girl I chanced to meet. Hi -
nice young man

94

MIDDLE
C
F# Gb
G# Ab
A# Bb
C# Db
D# Eb
F# Gb
G# Ab
C# Db
D# Eb
F G A B C D E F G A B C D E

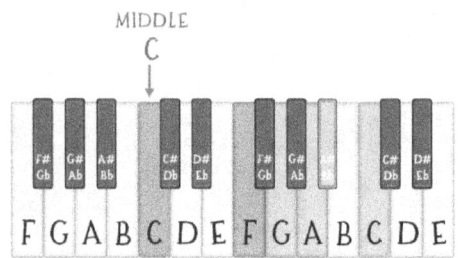

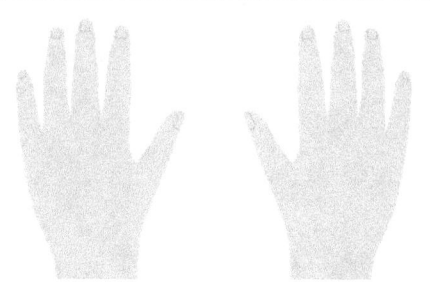

FIVE LITTLE DUCKS

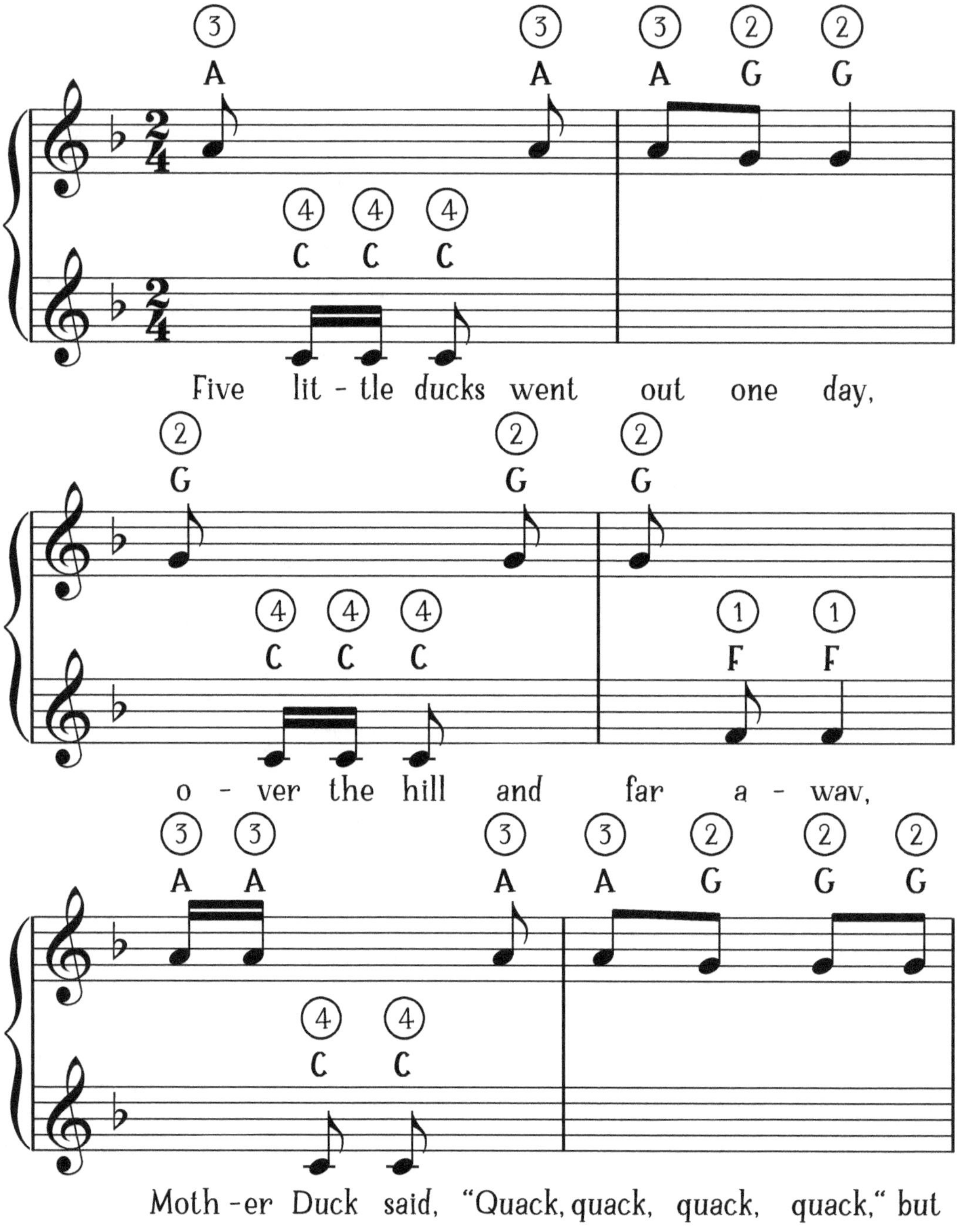

Five lit - tle ducks went out one day,
o - ver the hill and far a - way,
Moth -er Duck said, "Quack, quack, quack, quack," but

on - ly four lit - tle ducks came back.

2. Four little ducks…

3. Three little ducks…

4. Two little ducks…

5. One little duck went out one day,
   Over the hill and far away.
   Mother Duck said, "Quack, quack, quack, quack,"
   And all the five little ducks came back!

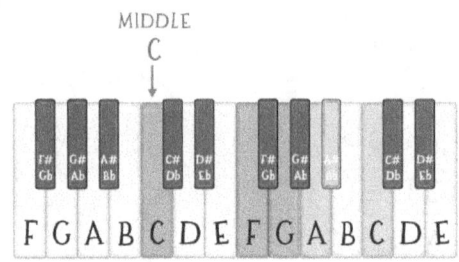

ITSY BITSY SPIDER

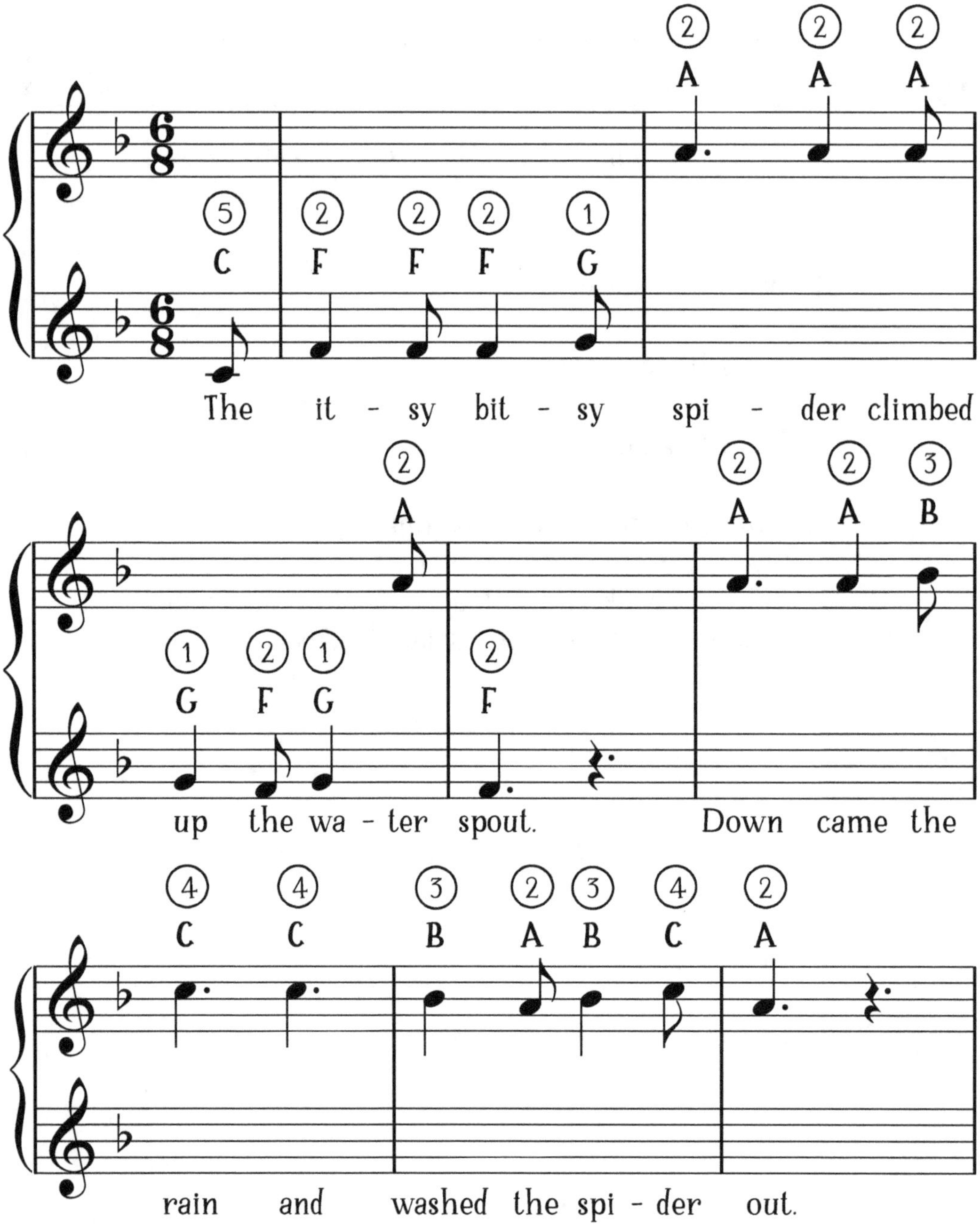

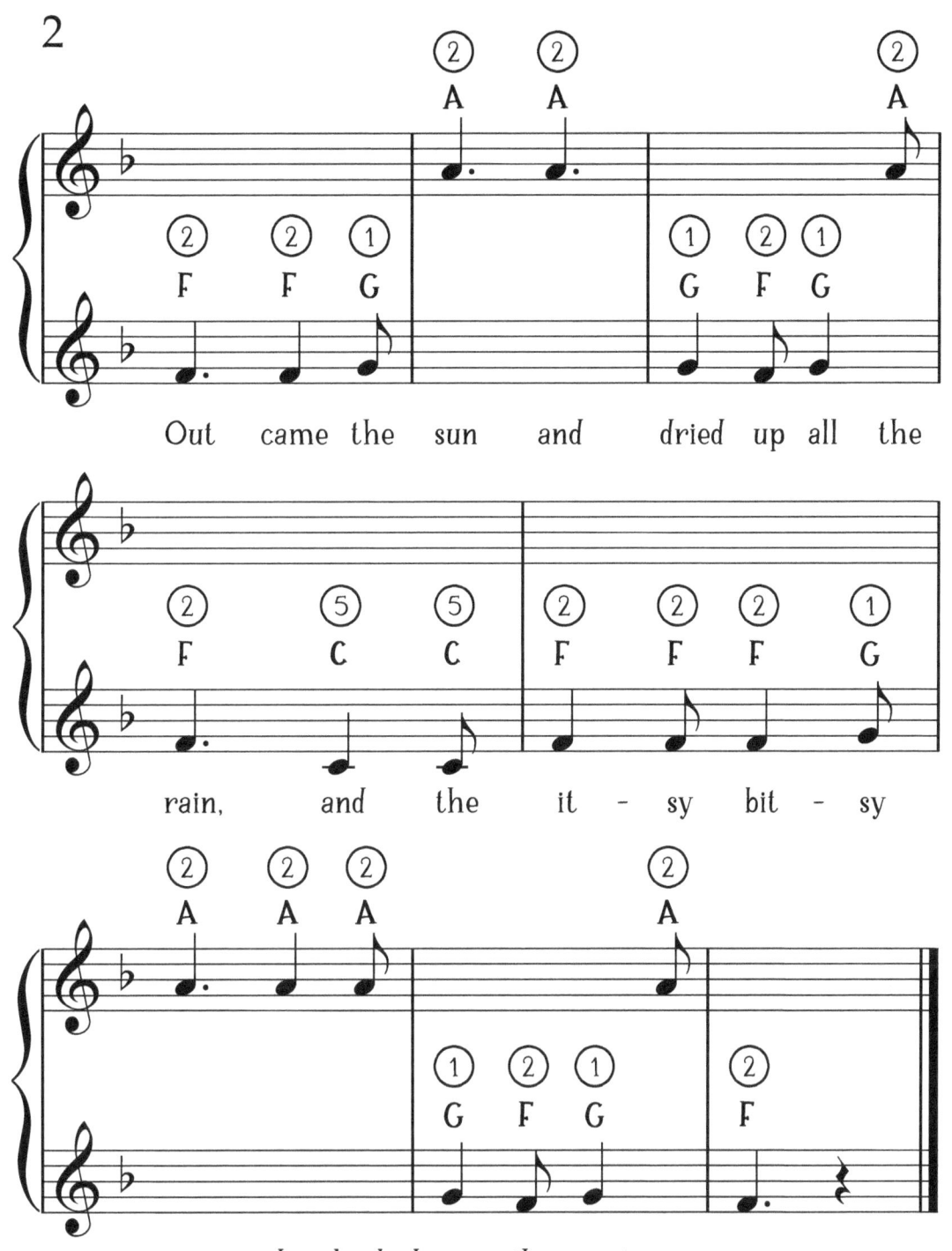

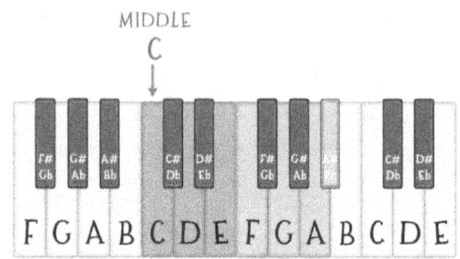
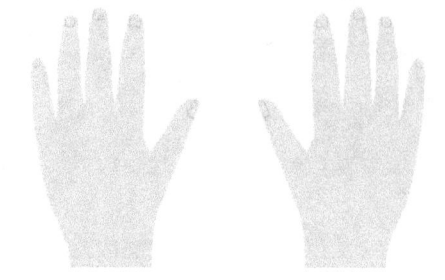

IF YOU'RE HAPPY AND YOU KNOW IT

② ② ② ② ② ② ②
F F F F F F F

④ ④ ②
C C E

If you're hap-py and you know it, clap your

③
G

④ ④
C C

hands (clap clap) If you're

③ ③ ③ ③ ③ ③ ② ③
G G G G G G F G

hap - py and you know it, clap your

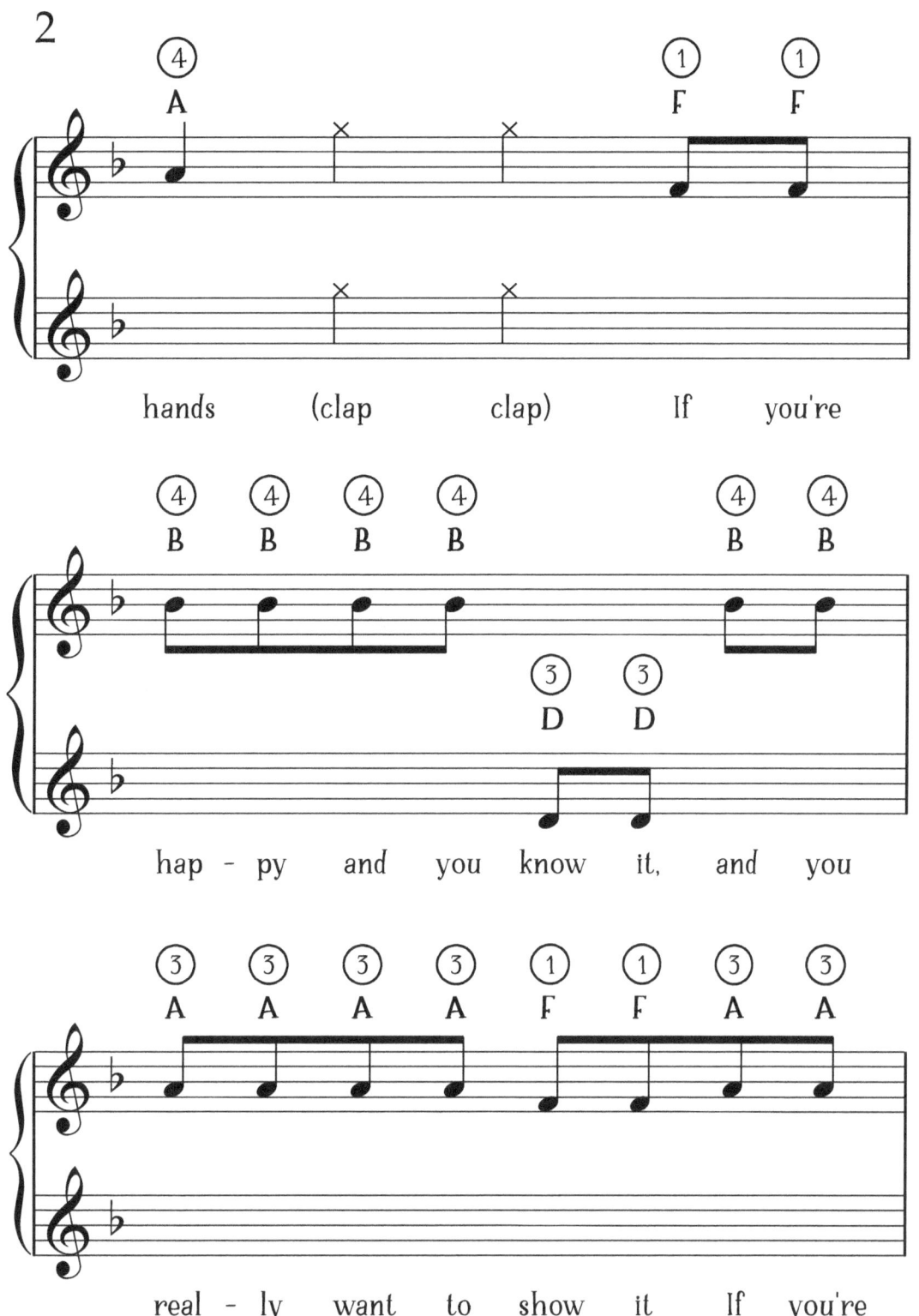

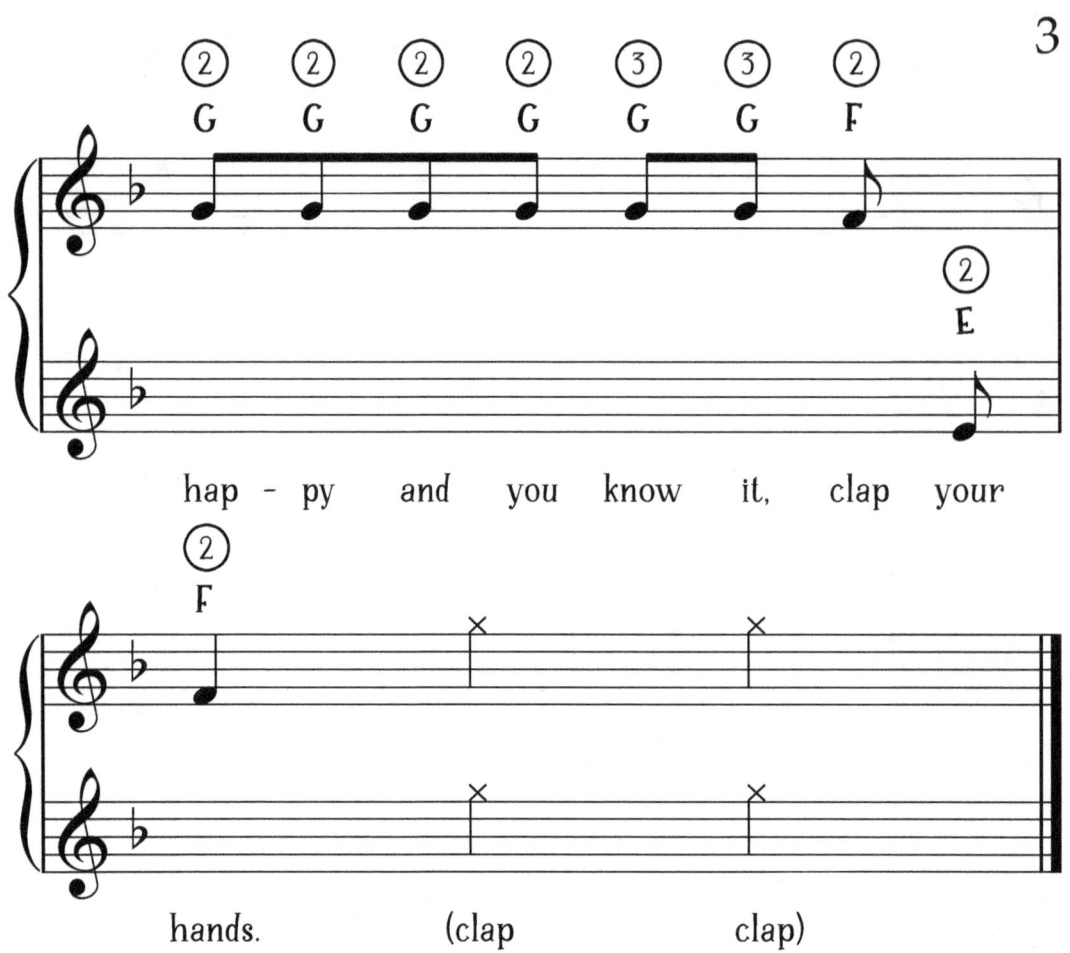

2. If you're happy and you know it,
   stomp your feet (stomp stomp)...

3. If you're happy and you know it,
   shout "Hurray!" (hoo-ray!)...

4. If you're happy and you know it,
   do all three (clap-clap, stomp-stomp, hoo-ray!)...

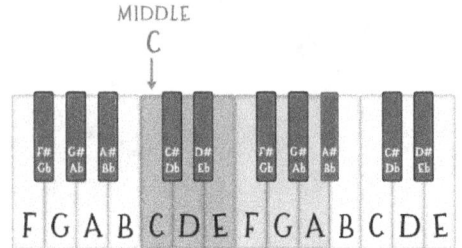
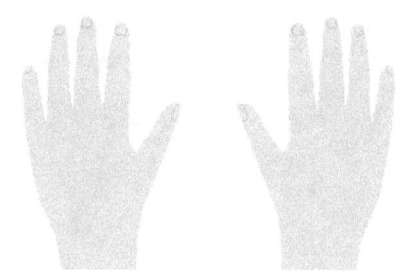

LONDON BRIDGE

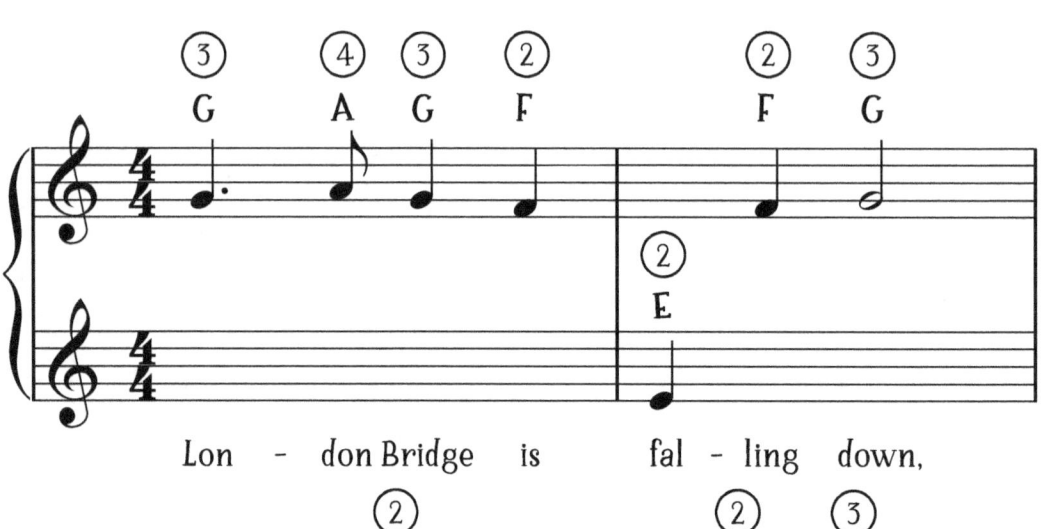

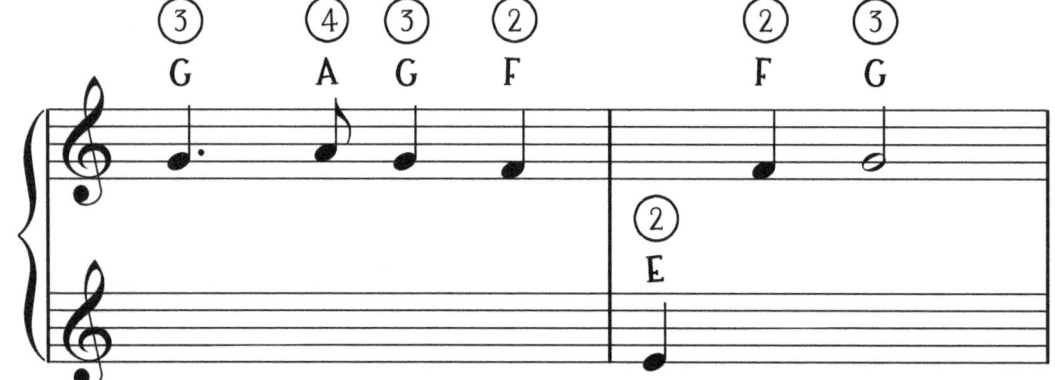

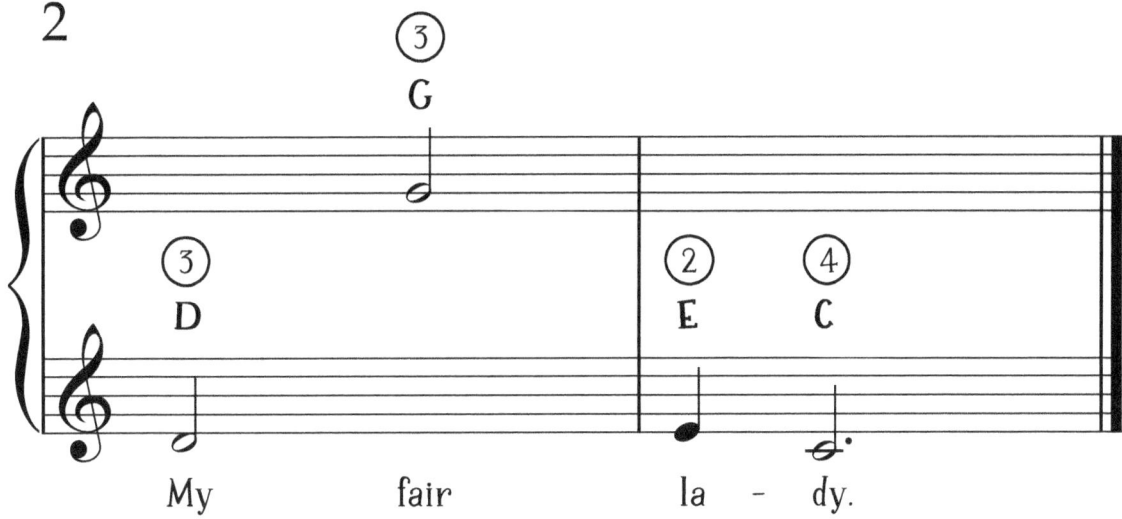

2. Build it up with iron bars...

3. Iron bars will bend and break...

4. Build it up with silver and gold...

Do you remember how the dot near the note head works? It makes the note last half as long. Before, we saw it in time signatures like 3/4 or 6/8, where notes needed to last for three notes instead of two.

This time, the dot will do the same thing, but to create an interesting rhythm. It helps make the song sound more fun and exciting!

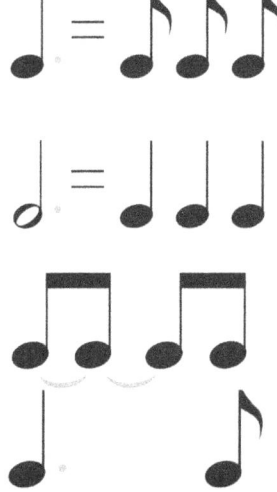

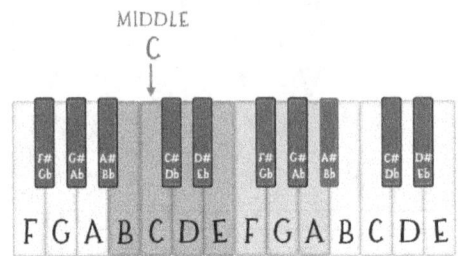
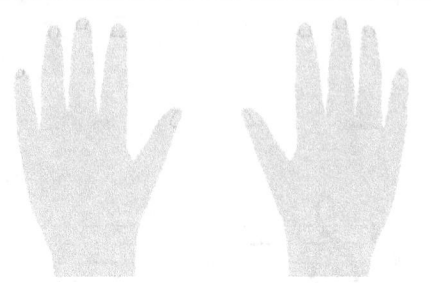

BLOW THE MAN DOWN

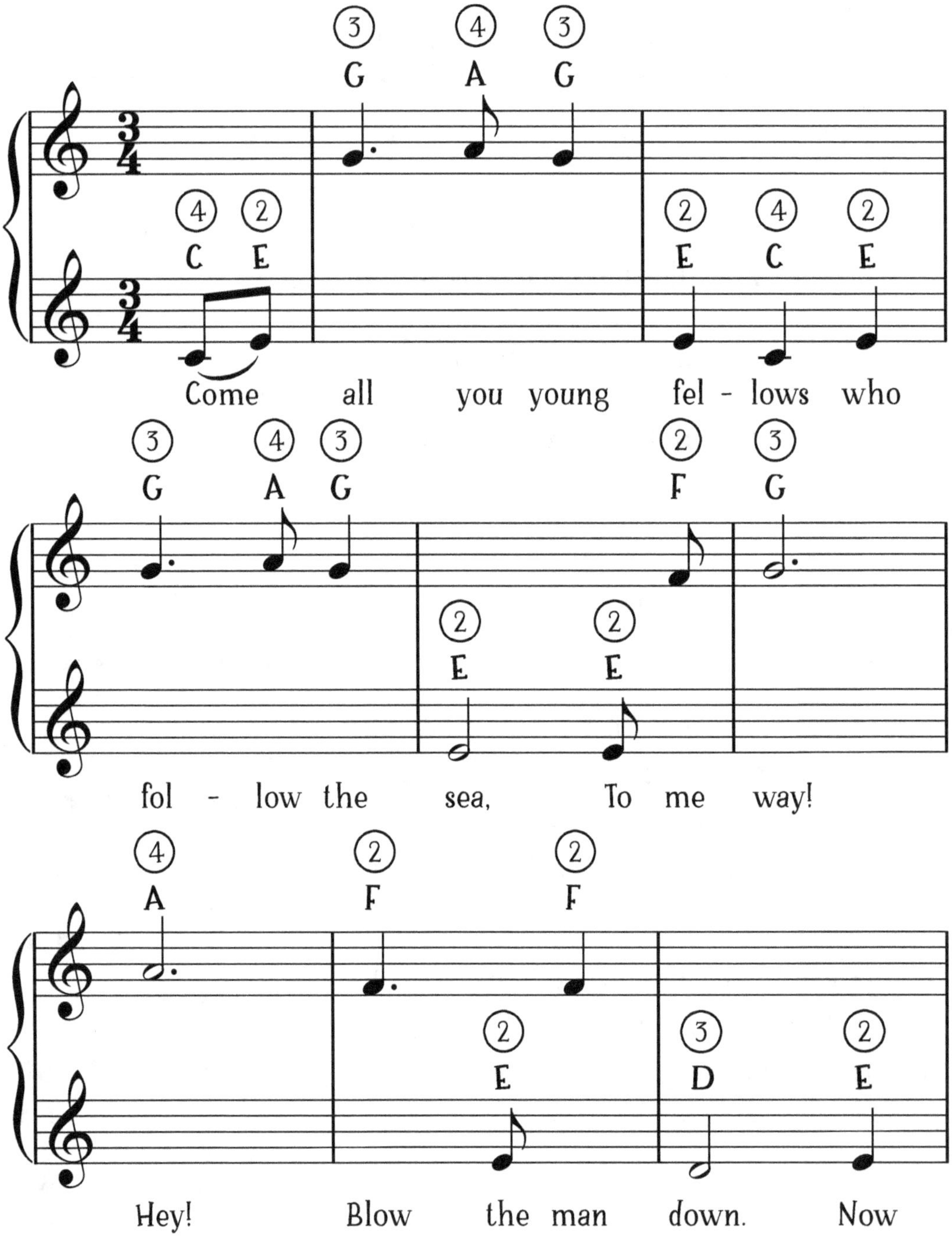

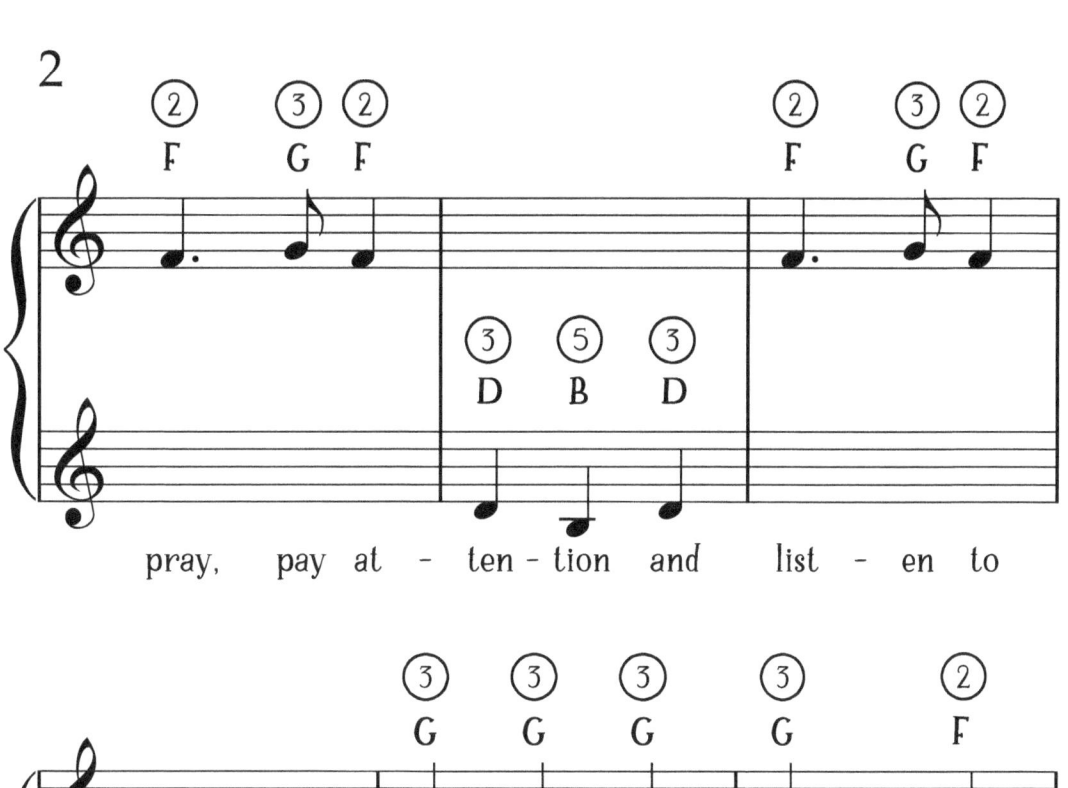
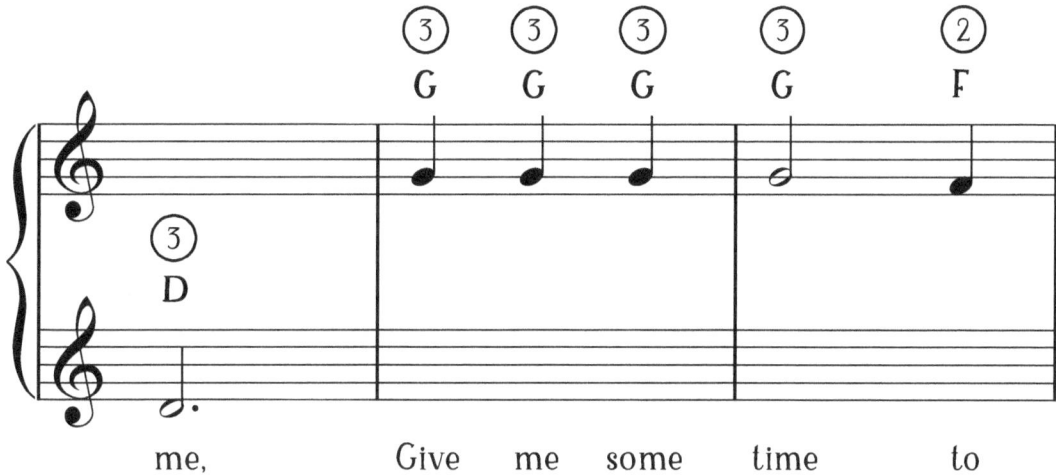
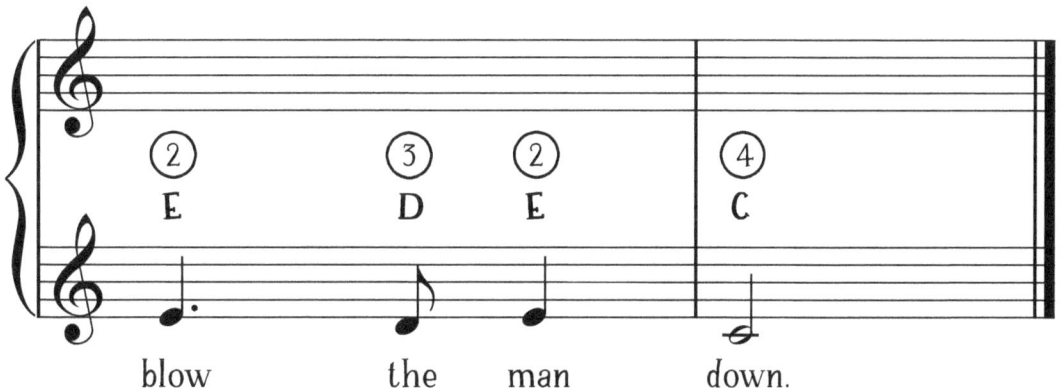

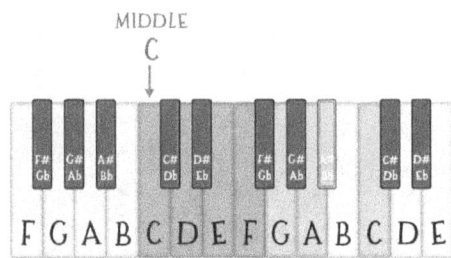

ORANGES AND LEMONS

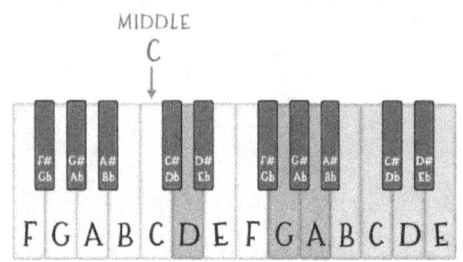

THE MORE WE GET TOGETHER

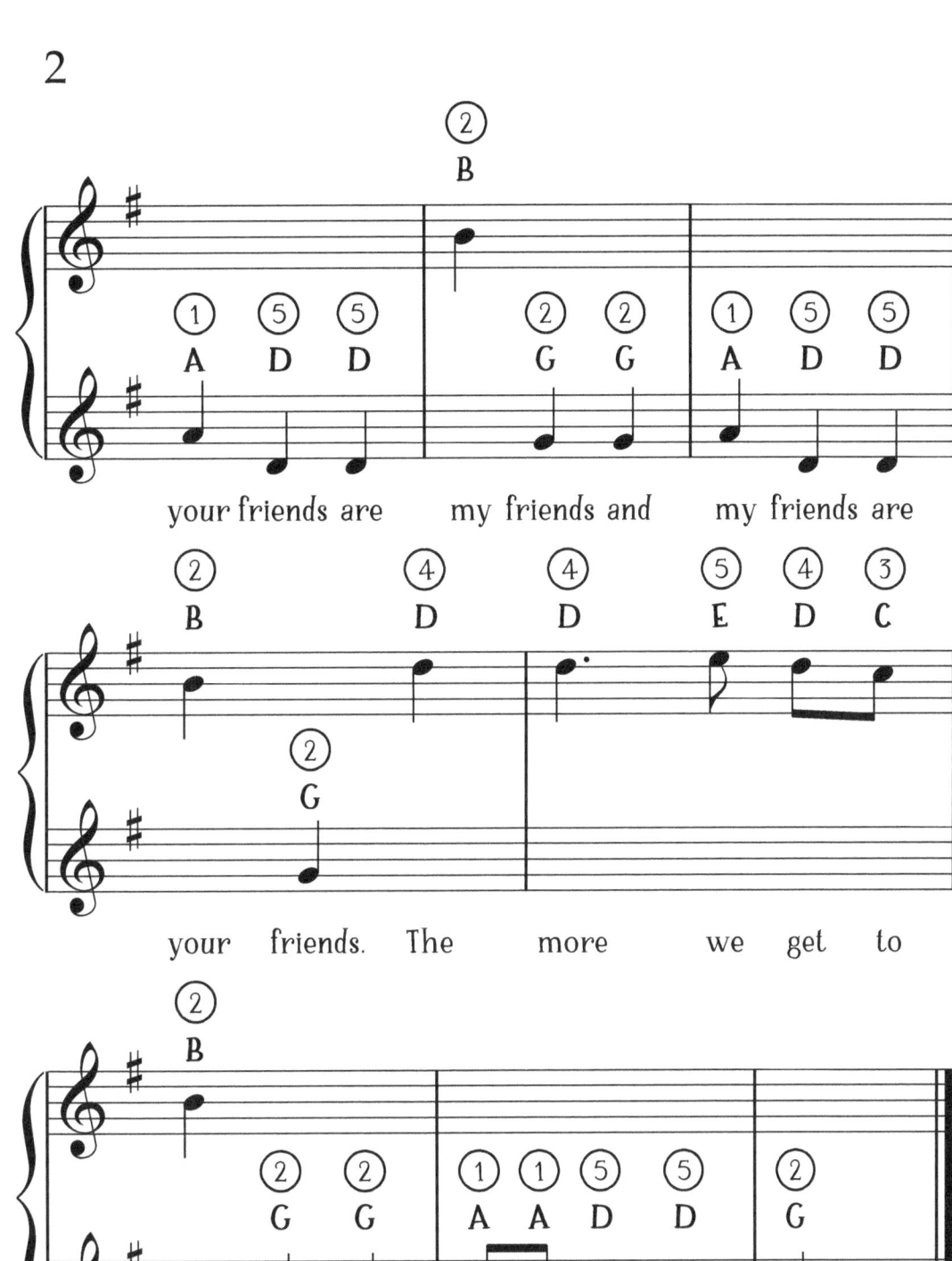

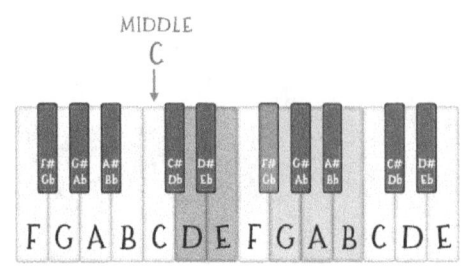
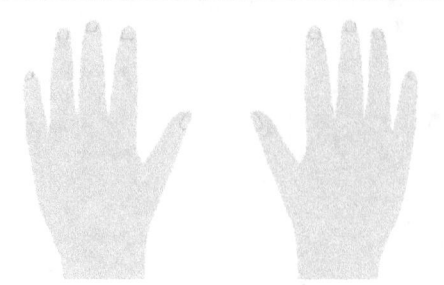

THE MUFFIN MAN

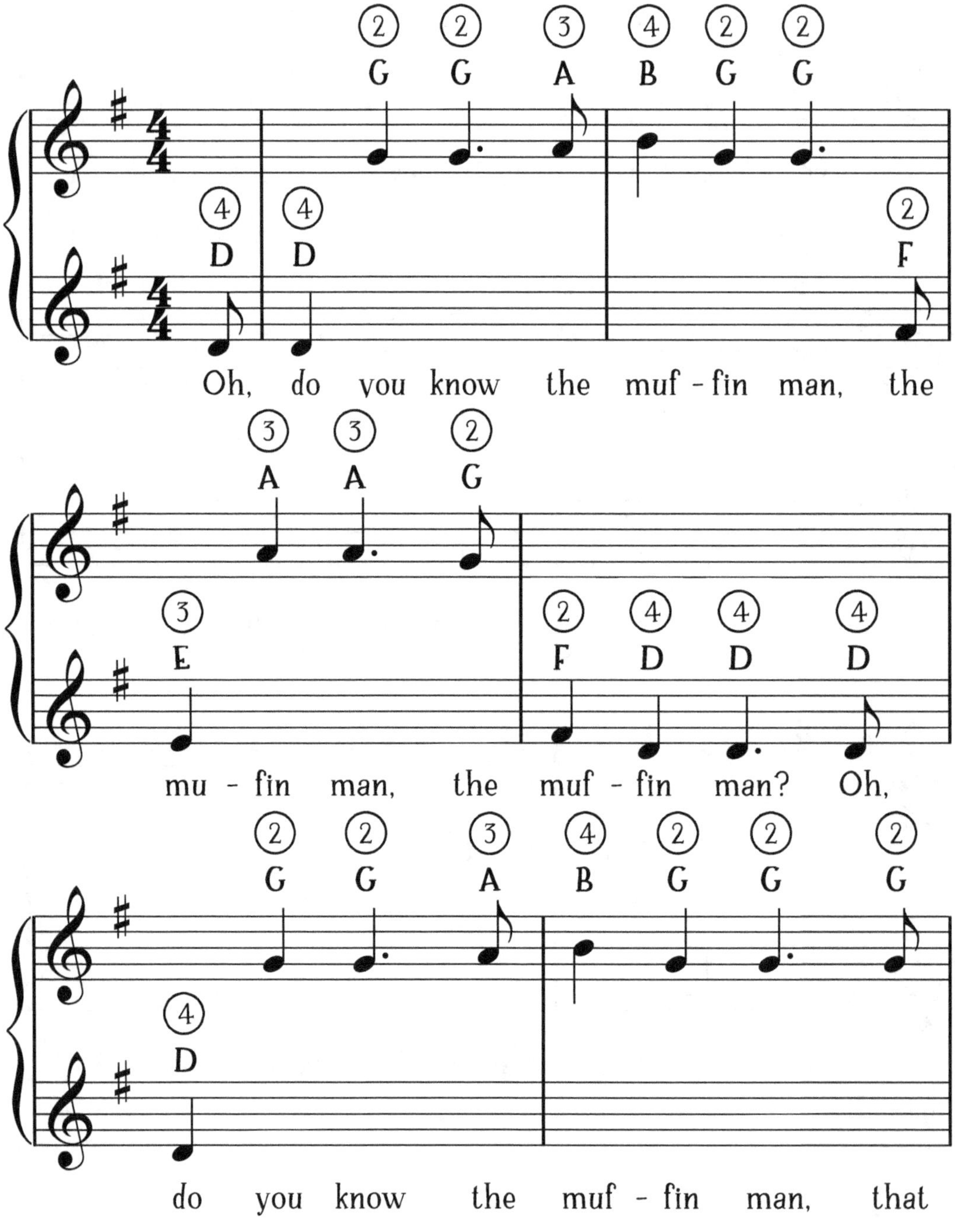

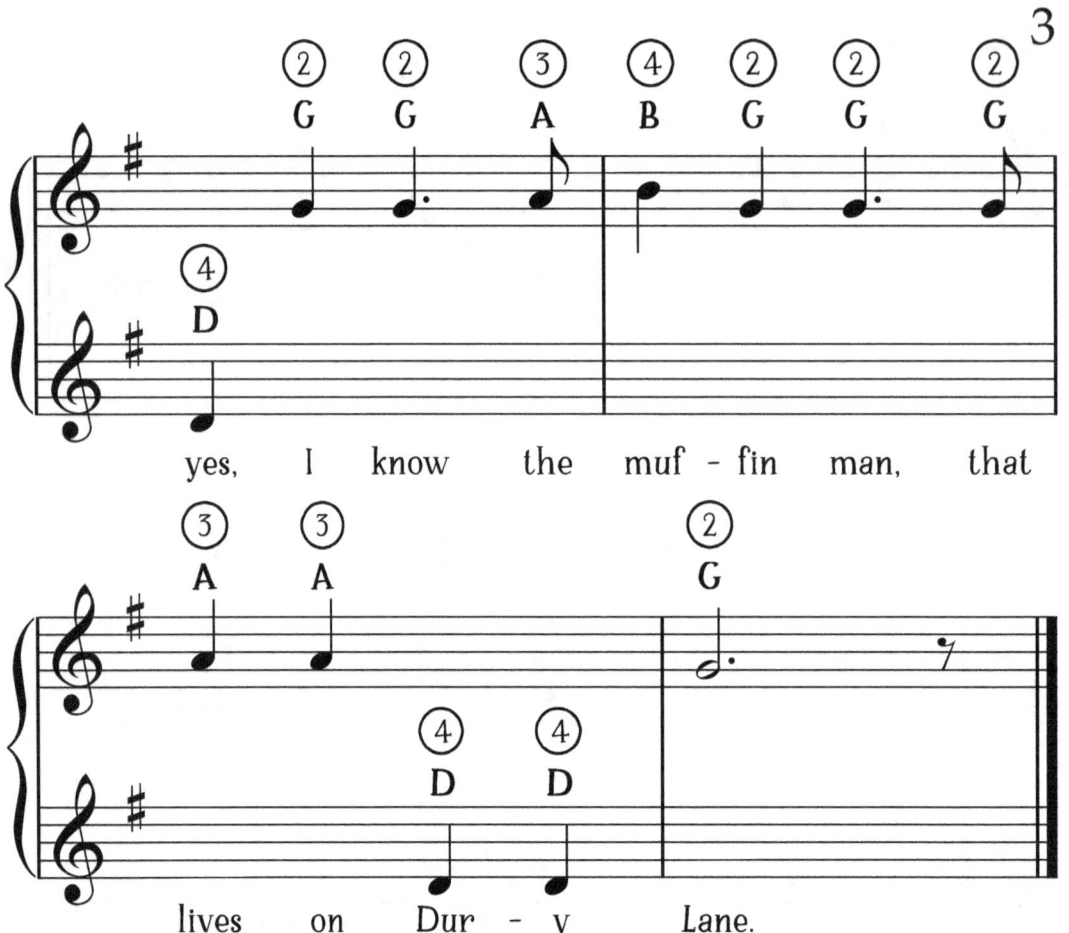

2. Now, two of us know the muffin man,
   The muffin man, the muffin man,
   Oh, two of us know the muffin man,
   Who lives in Drury Lane.

3. A few of us know the muffin man,
   The muffin man, the muffin man,
   A few of us know the muffin man,
   Who lives in Drury Lane.

4. Now we all know the muffin man,
   The muffin man, the muffin man,
   Now we all know the muffin man,
   Who lives in Drury Lane.

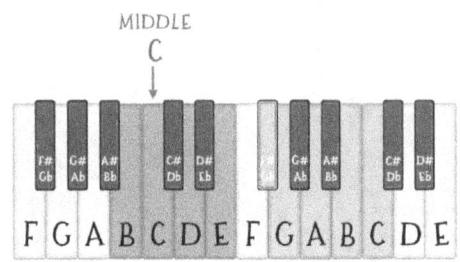

ROCK-A-BYE BABY

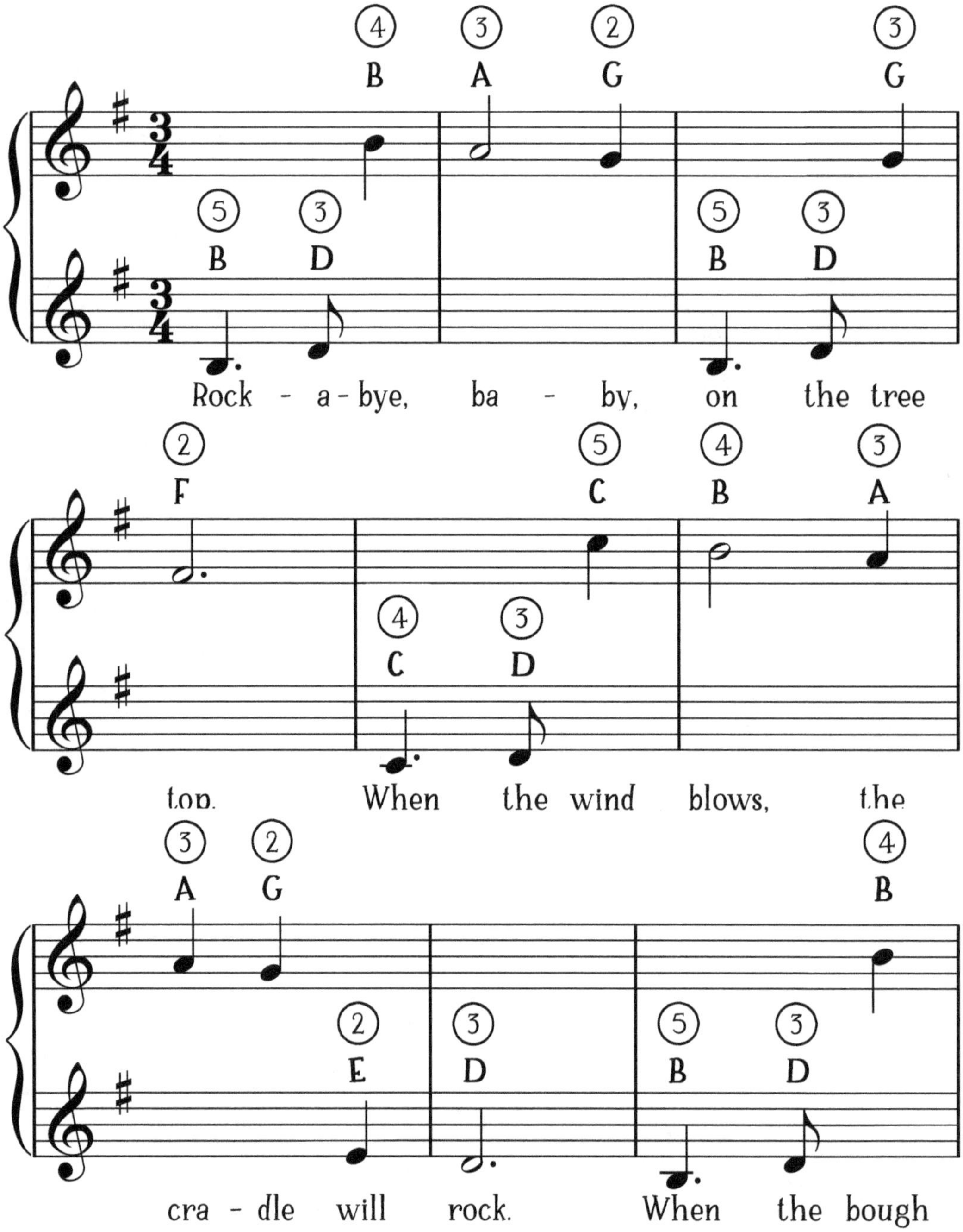

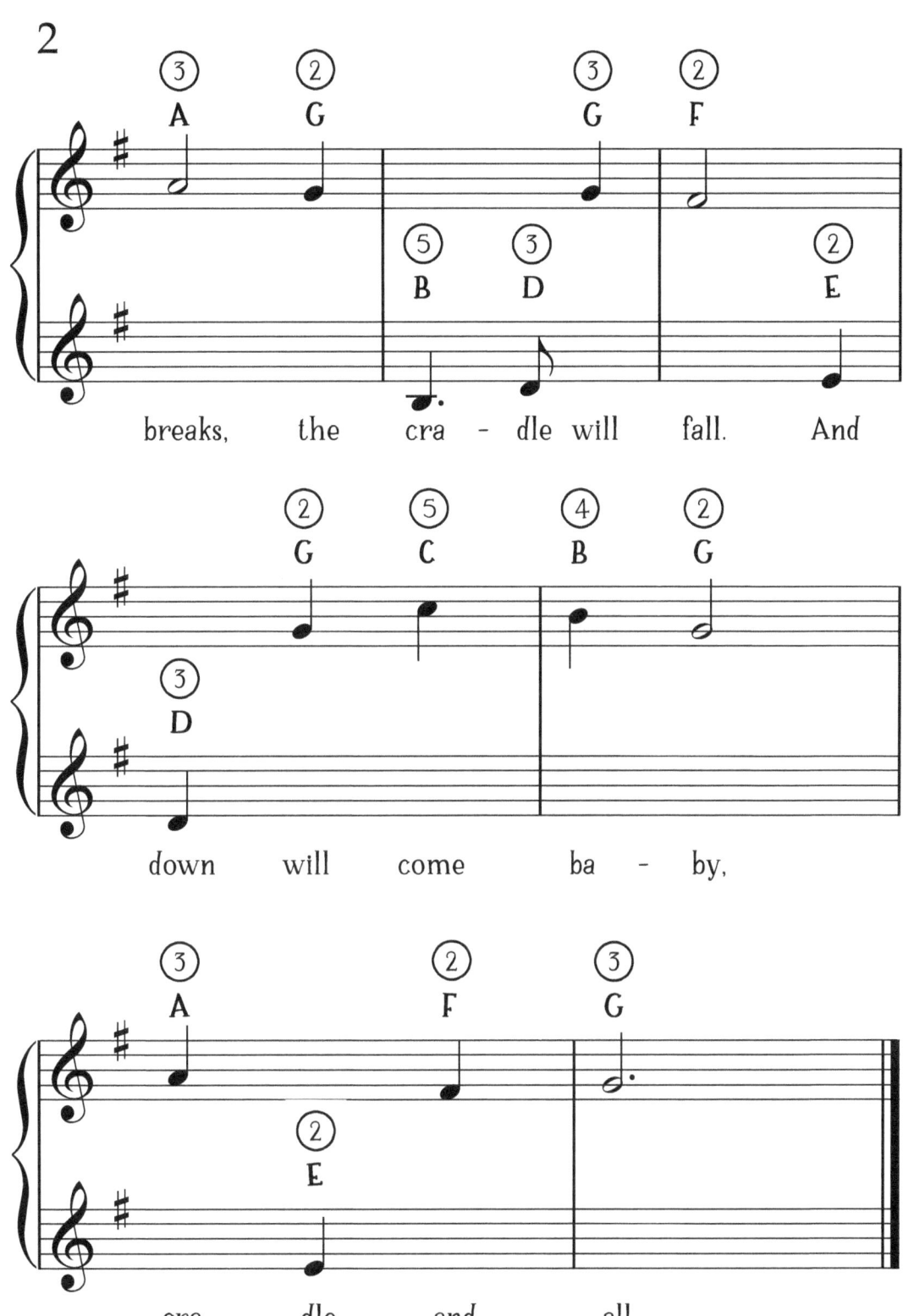

CHAPTER 5

MIDDLE
C
F G A B C D E F G A B C D E

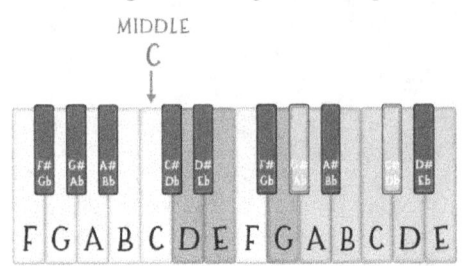

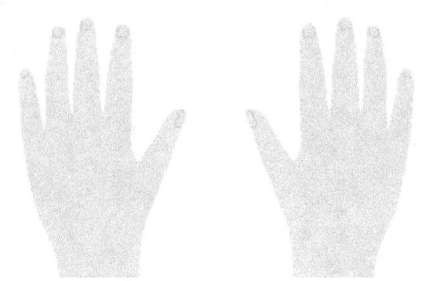

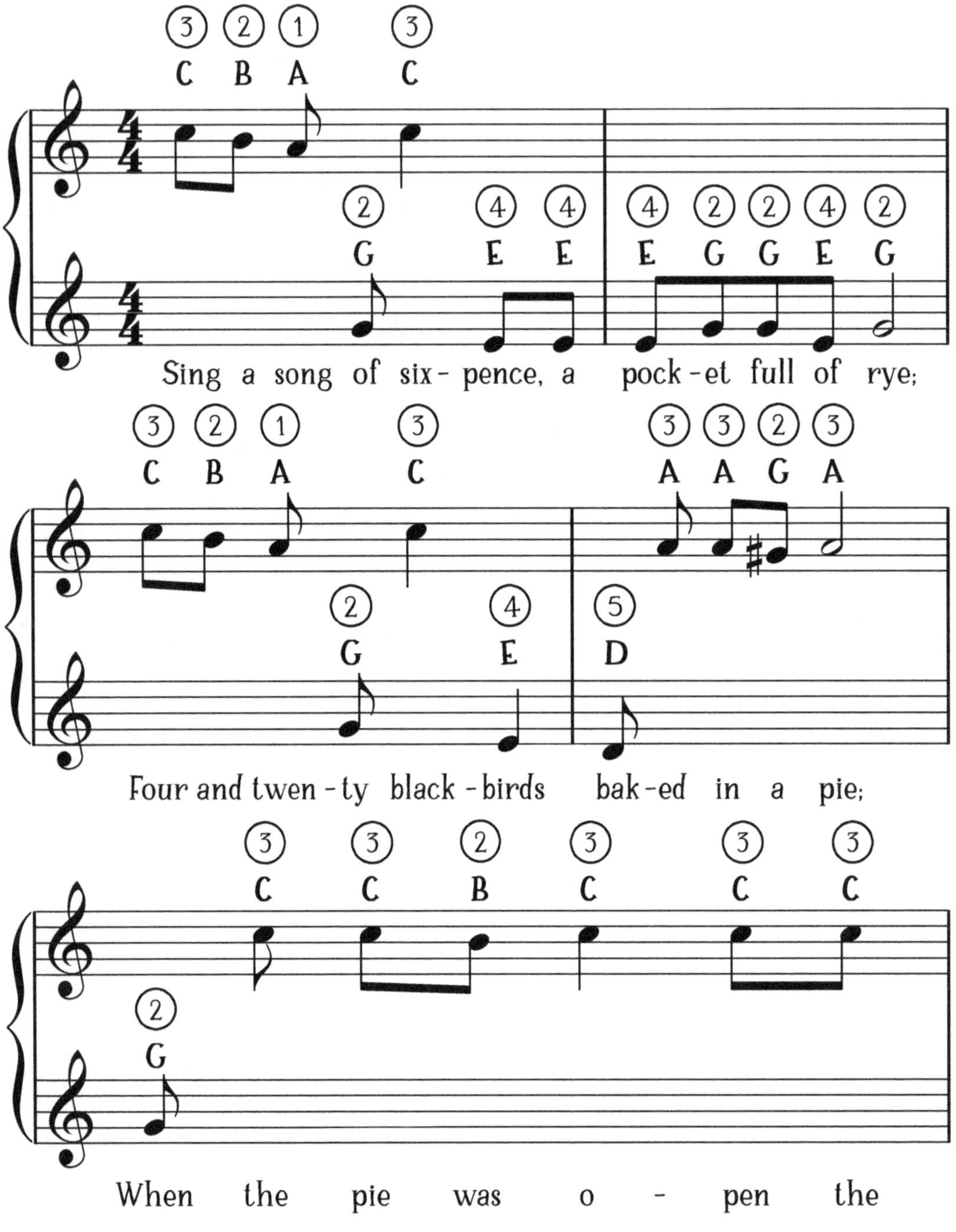

SING A SONG OF SIXPENCE

C B A C
G E E E G G E G
Sing a song of six- pence, a pock - et full of rye;
C B A C A A G A
G E D
Four and twen - ty black - birds bak - ed in a pie;
C C B C C C
G
When the pie was o - pen the

2. The king was in his counting-house
counting out his money;
The queen was in the parlor eating bread and honey;
The maid was in the garden hanging out her clothes,
When up came a blackbird and pecked off her nose!

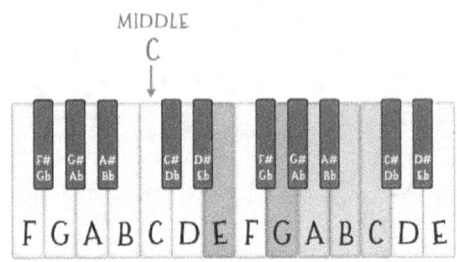
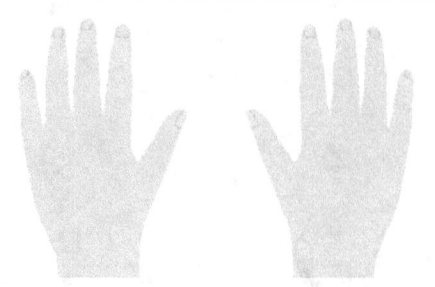

THE ANIMAL FAIR

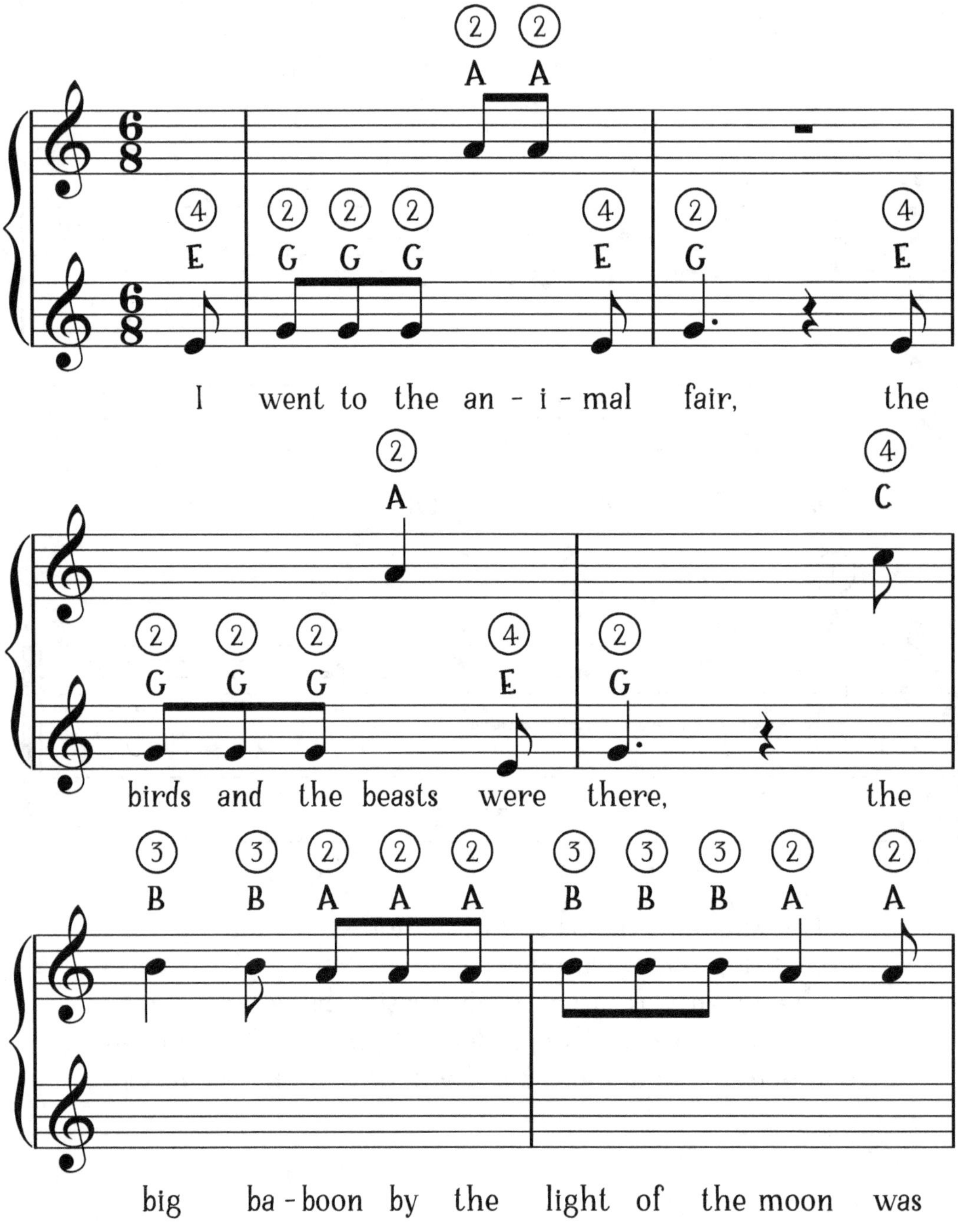

I went to the an-i-mal fair, the birds and the beasts were there, the big ba-boon by the light of the moon was

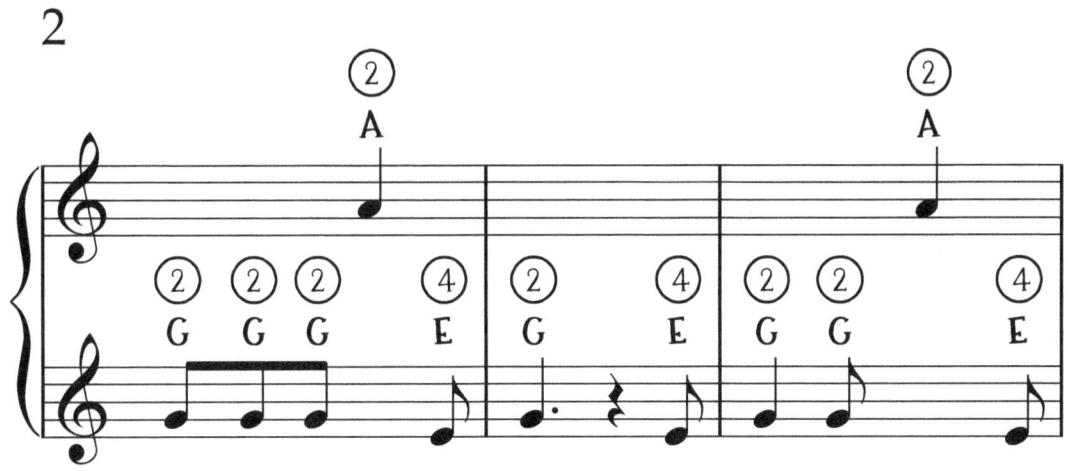
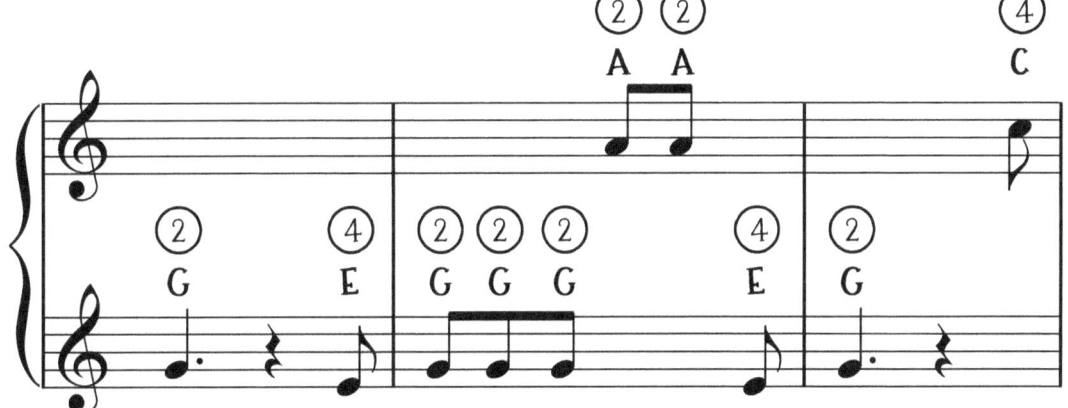
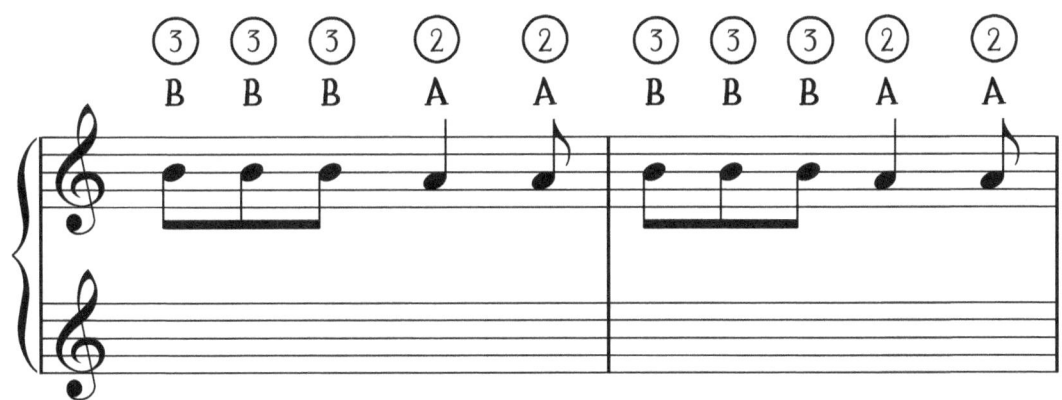

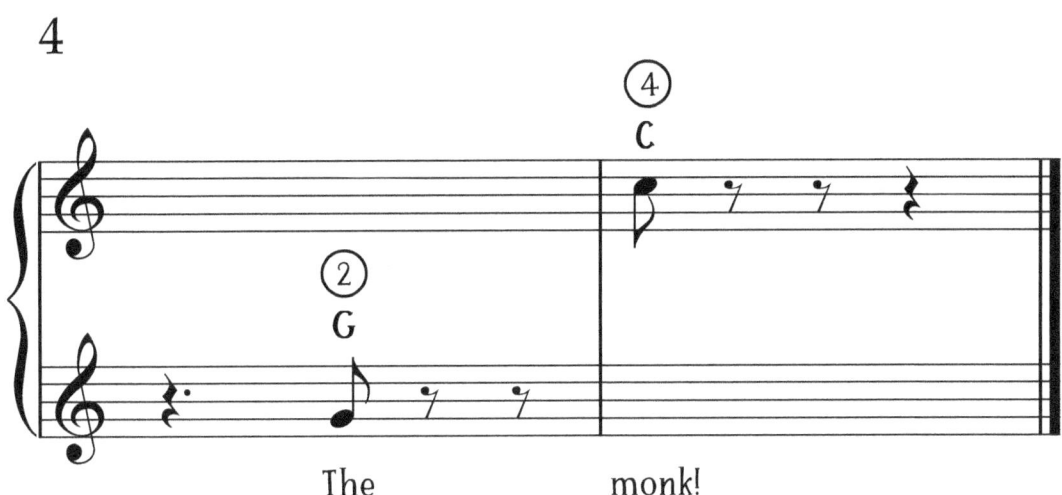

MIDDLE
C
F# Gb
G# Ab
A# Bb
C# Db
D# Eb
F# Gb
G# Ab
A# Bb
C# Db
D# Eb
F G A B C D E F G A B C D E

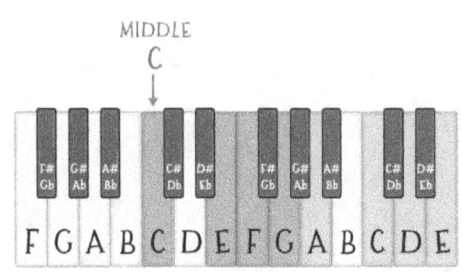

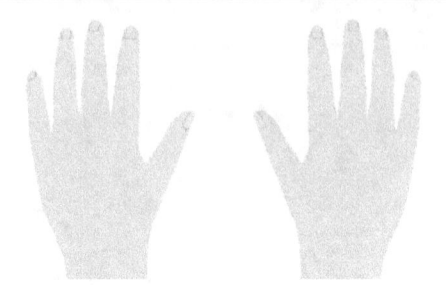

A JOLLY FAT FROG LIVED IN THE RIVER

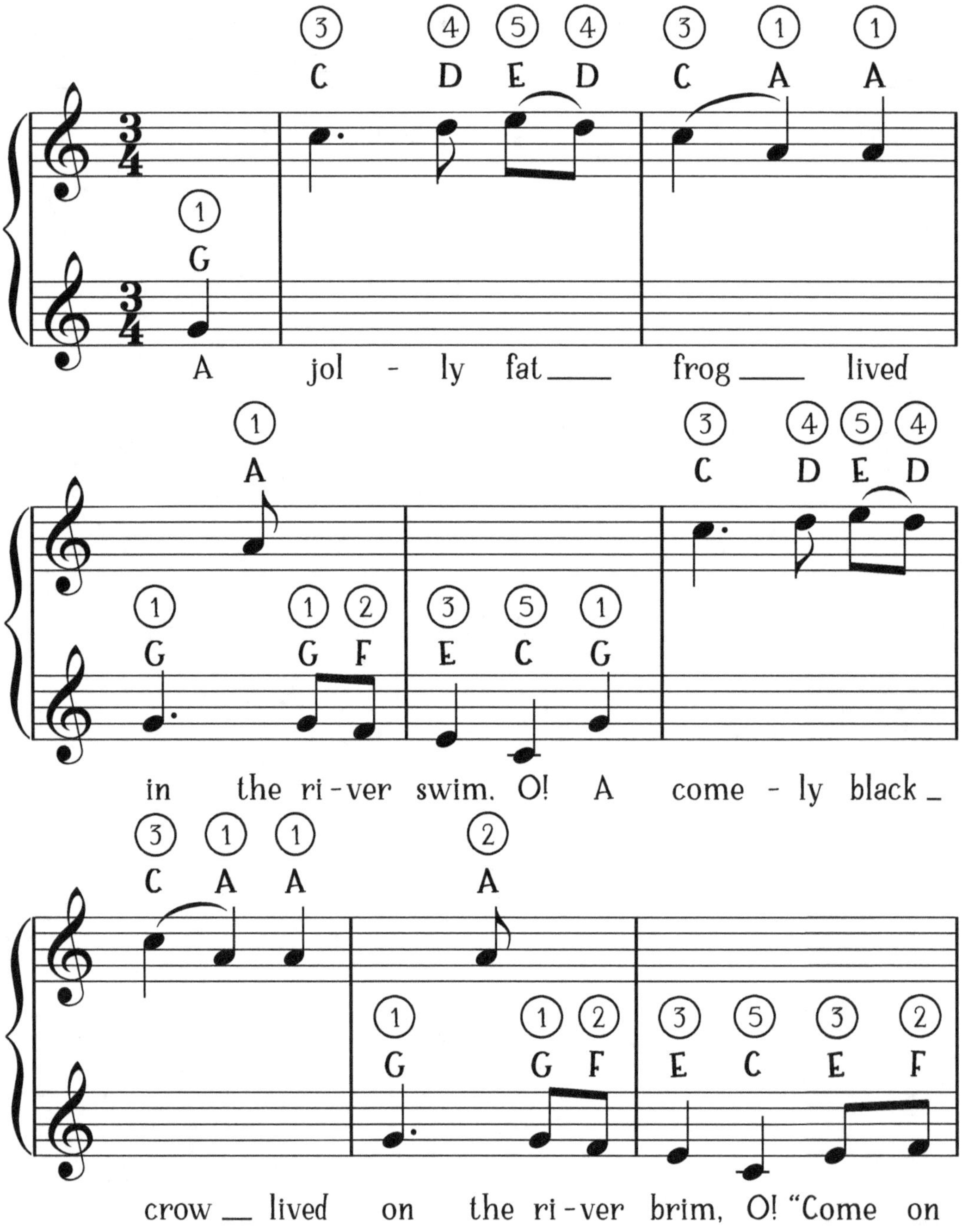

3 4 5 4 3 1 1
C D E D C A A
1
G
A jol - ly fat ___ frog ___ lived
1 3 4 5 4
A C D E D
1 1 2 3 5 1
G G F E C G
in the ri - ver swim, O! A come - ly black ___
3 1 1 2
C A A A
1 1 2 3 5 3 2
G G F E C E F
crow ___ lived on the ri - ver brim, O! "Come on

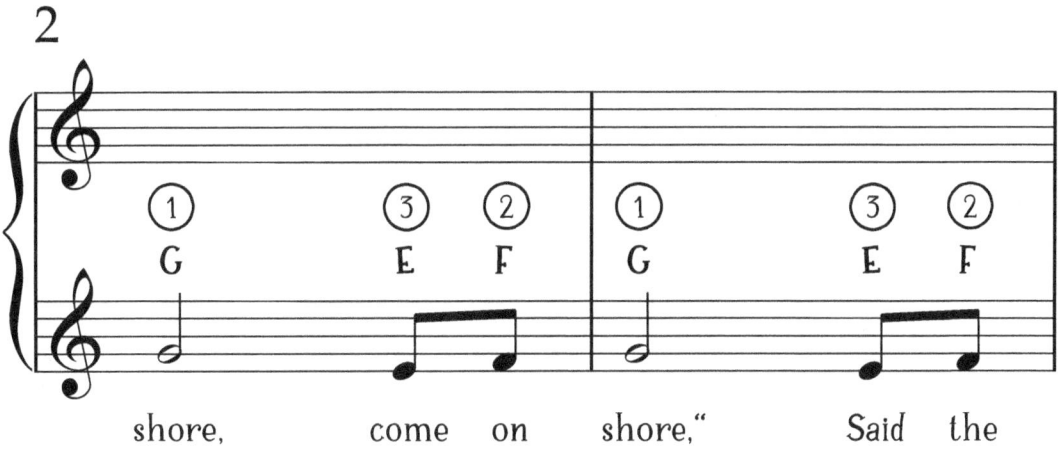
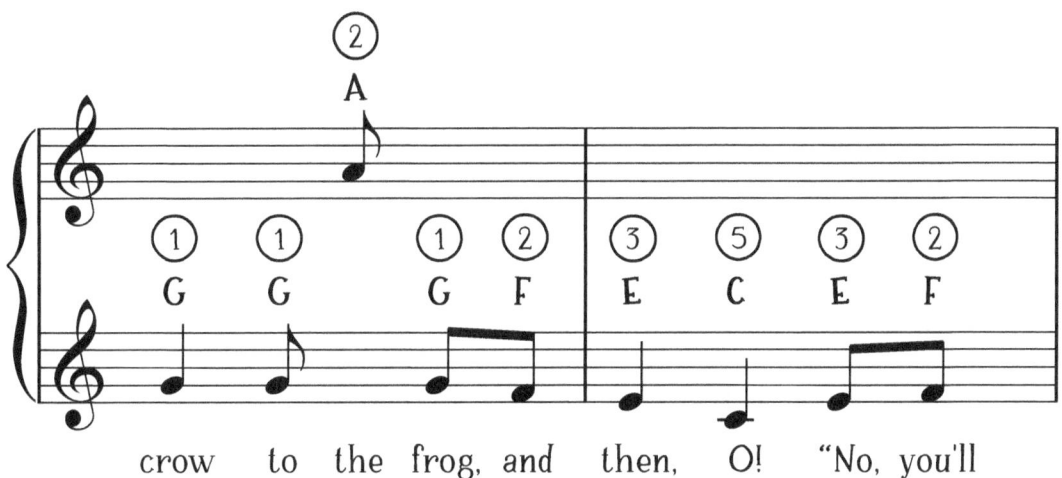
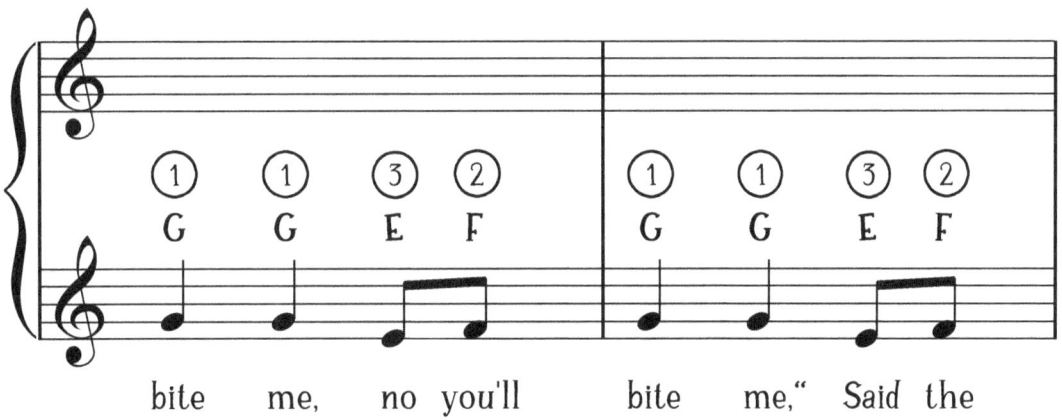

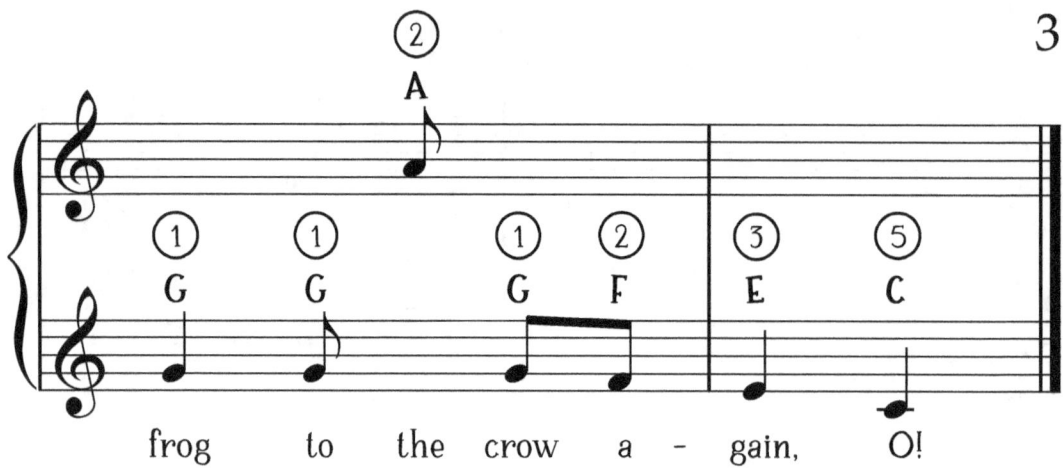

frog   to   the   crow   a - gain,   O!

2. "O! there is sweet music on yonder green hill, O!
   And you shall be a dancer, a dancer in yellow,
   All in yellow, all in yellow."
   Said the crow to the frog, and then, O!
   "All in yellow, all in yellow,"
   Said the frog to the crow again, O!

3. "Farewell, ye little fishes, that in the river swim, O!
   I'm going to be a dancer, a dancer in yellow."
   "O beware! O beware!"
   Said the fish to the frog, and then, O!
   "I'll take care, I'll take care,"
   Said the frog to the fish again, O!

4. The frog began a swimming, a swimming to land, O!
   And the crow began jumping to give him his hand, O!
   "Sir, you're welcome, Sir, you're welcome,"
   Said the crow to the frog, and then, O!
   "Sir, I thank you, Sir, I thank you,"
   Said the frog to the crow, again, O!

5. "But where is the sweet music on yonder green hill, O?
   And where are all the dancers, the dancers in yellow?
   All in yellow, all in yellow?"
   Said the frog to the crow, and then, O!
   "Sir, they're here, Sir, they're here."
   Said the crow to the frog*

*Here the crow swallows the frog.

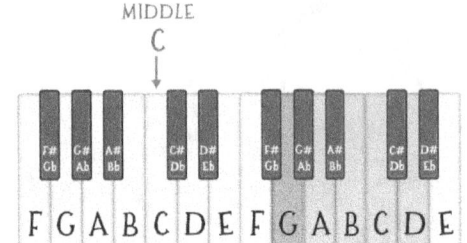

Helpful tip at the end of the song!

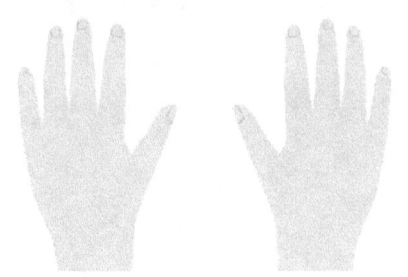

RING-A-RING ROSES

B B A C B A
A ring - a-ring o' ro - ses, A

B B A C B A D A
po - cket full of po - sies A - tish - oo, a-

D A B A
tish - oo We all fall down.

Here's another dotter rhythm, like the ones we've seen before with eighths and quarters. This time, it's with sixteenths and eighth notes. This rhythm sounds a bit faster and sharper.

Imagine that you're resting on the eighth note with dots for a little while, and

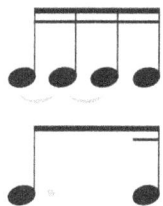

then, suddenly, the sixteenth note comes quickly at the last minute.

This rhythm makes the music sound lively and exciting!

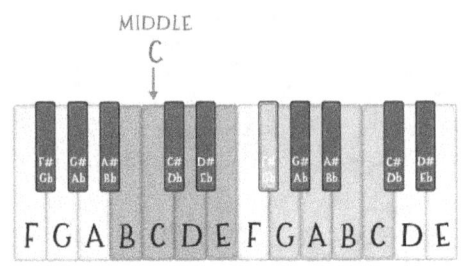

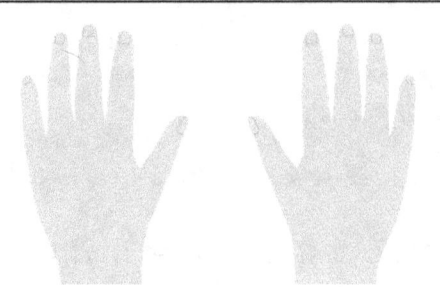

MIDDLE
C
F# Gb
G# Ab
A# Bb
C# Db
D# Eb
F# Gb
G# Ab
A# Bb
C# Db
D# Eb
F G A B C D E F G A B C D E

YANKEE DOODLE

1 1 2 3 1 3 2
G G A B G B A
3
D
Yan - kee Doo - dle went to town, a -
1 1 2 3 1 2
G G A B G F
rid - ing on a pon - y.
1 1 2 3 4 3 2 1
G G A B C B A G
Stuck a feath - er in his cap and

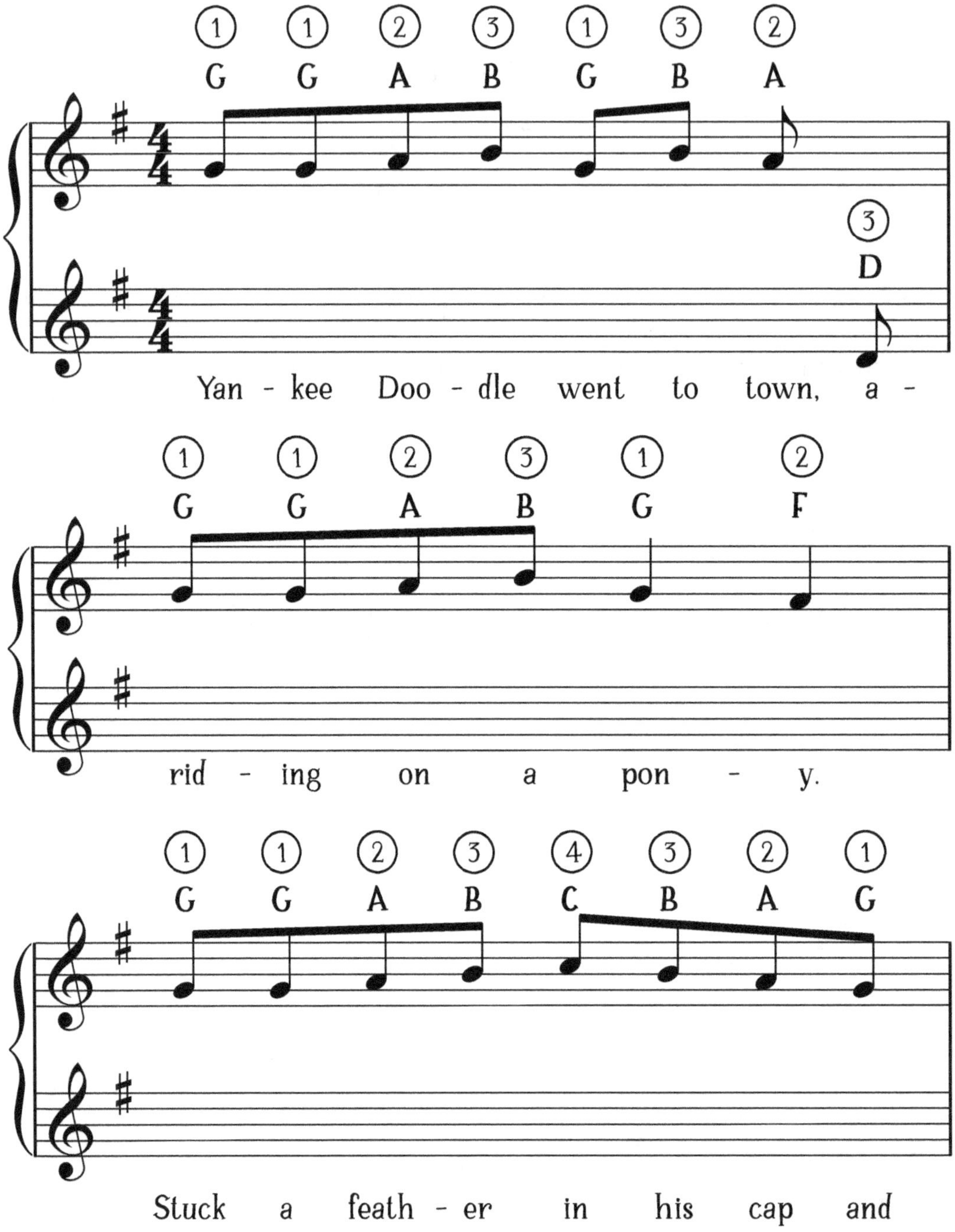

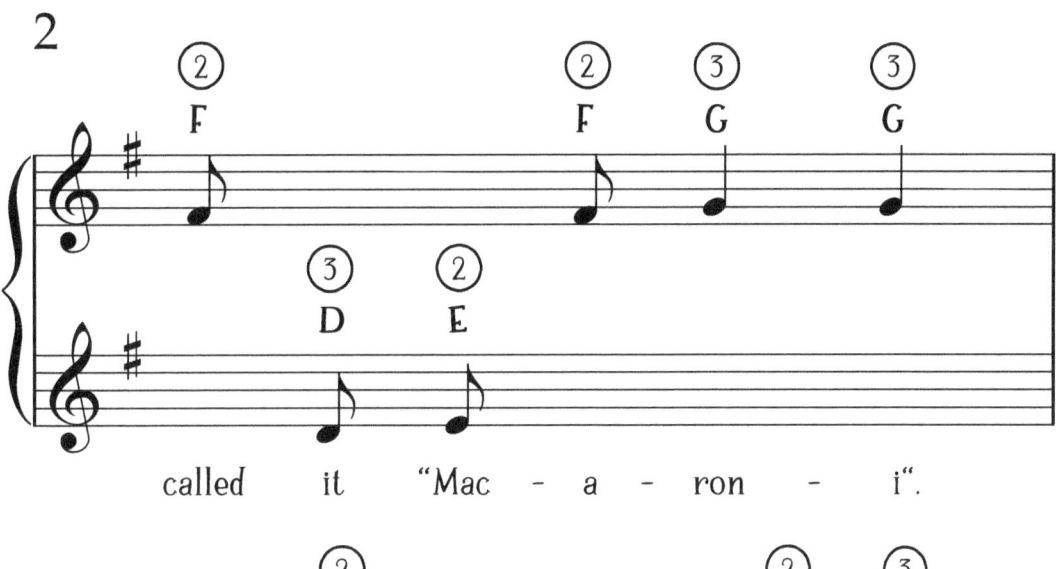
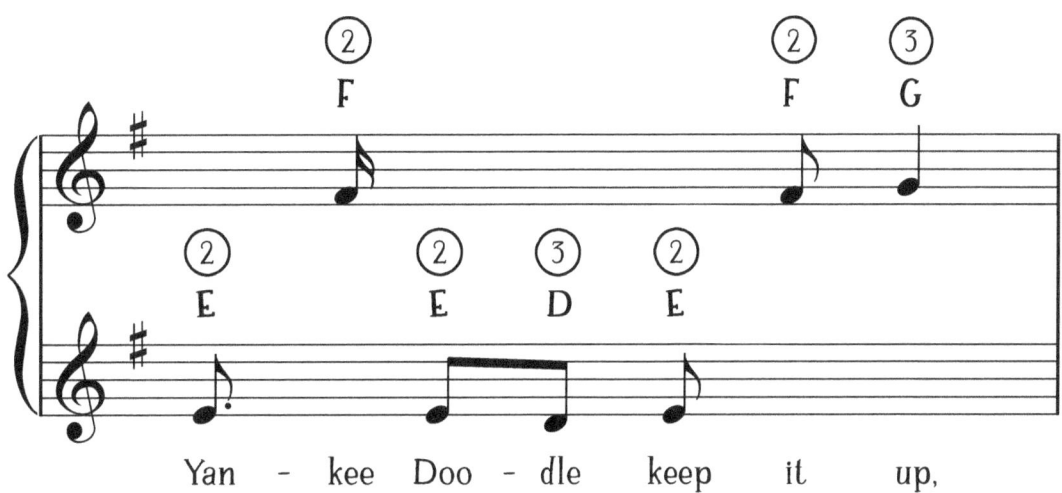
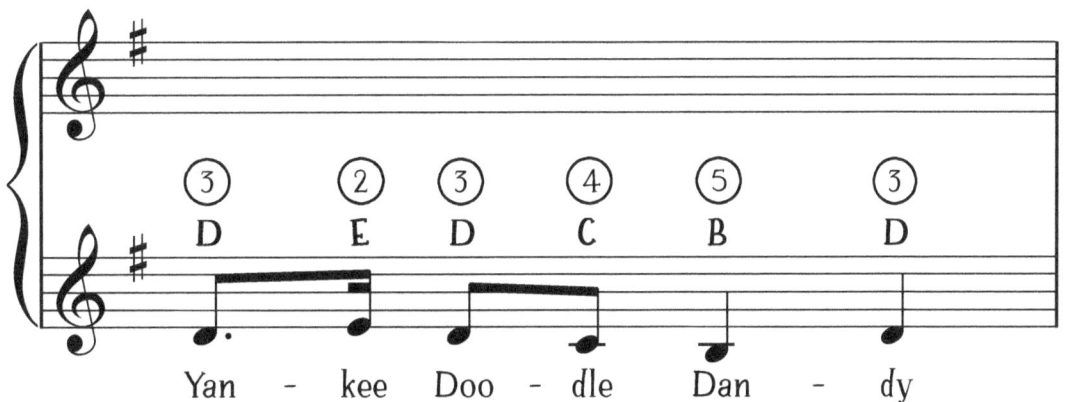

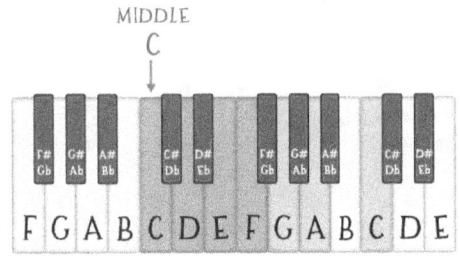
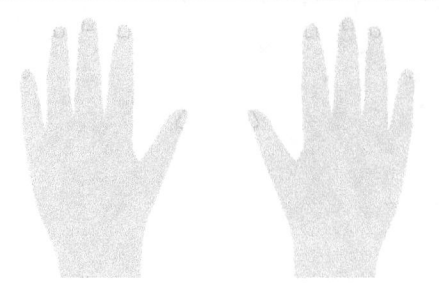

MICHAEL FINNEGAN

There was a man named Mi-chael Fin-ne-gan,

He had whis-kers on his chin-ne-gan,

They fell out and then grew back a-gain,

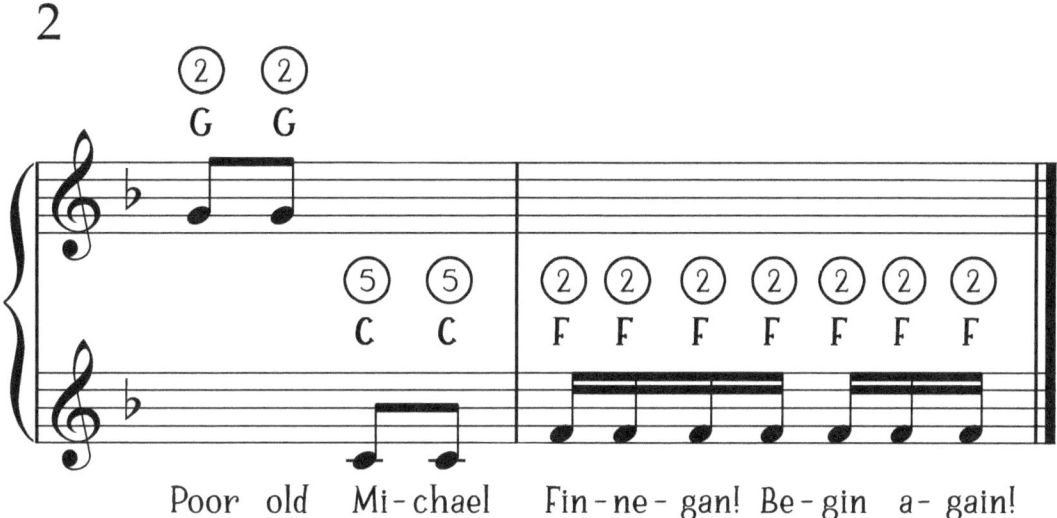

2. There was a man named Michael Finnegan,
   He went fishing with a pinnegan,
   Caught a fish and dropped it in again,
   Poor old Michael Finnegan! Begin again!

3. There was a man named Michael Finnegan,
   He grew fat and then grew thin again,
   Then he died, and had to begin again,
   Poor old Michael Finnegan! Begin again!

MIDDLE
C
F G A B C D E F G A B C D E

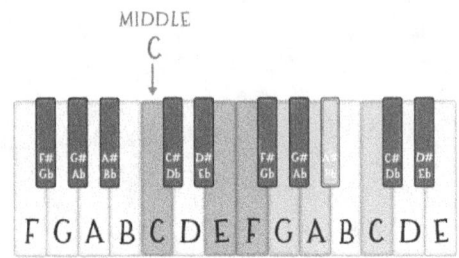

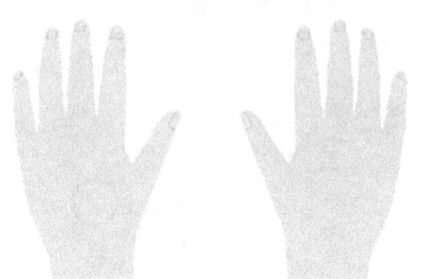

CLEMENTINE

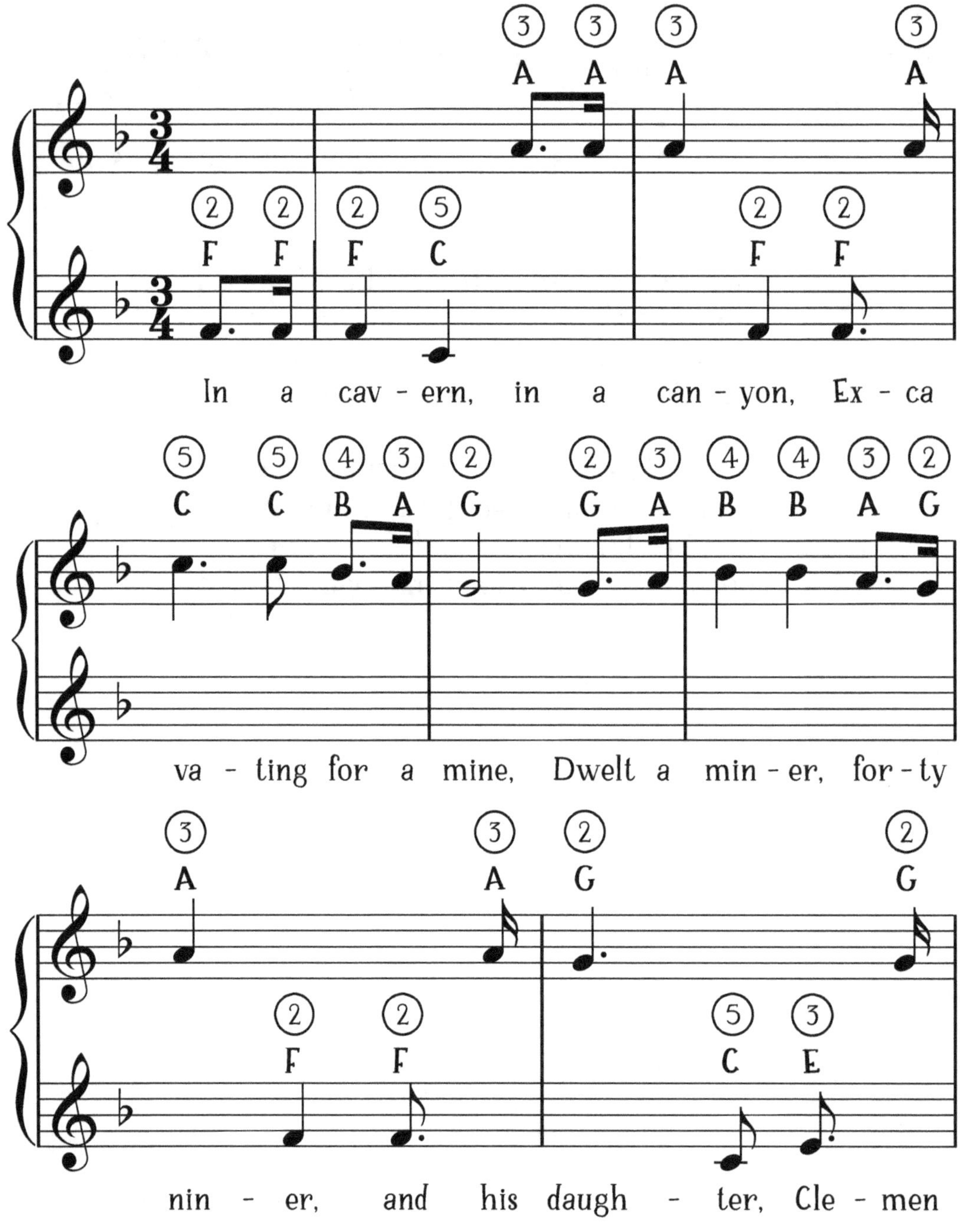

In a cav - ern, in a can - yon, Ex - ca
va - ting for a mine, Dwelt a min - er, for - ty
nin - er, and his daugh - ter, Cle - men

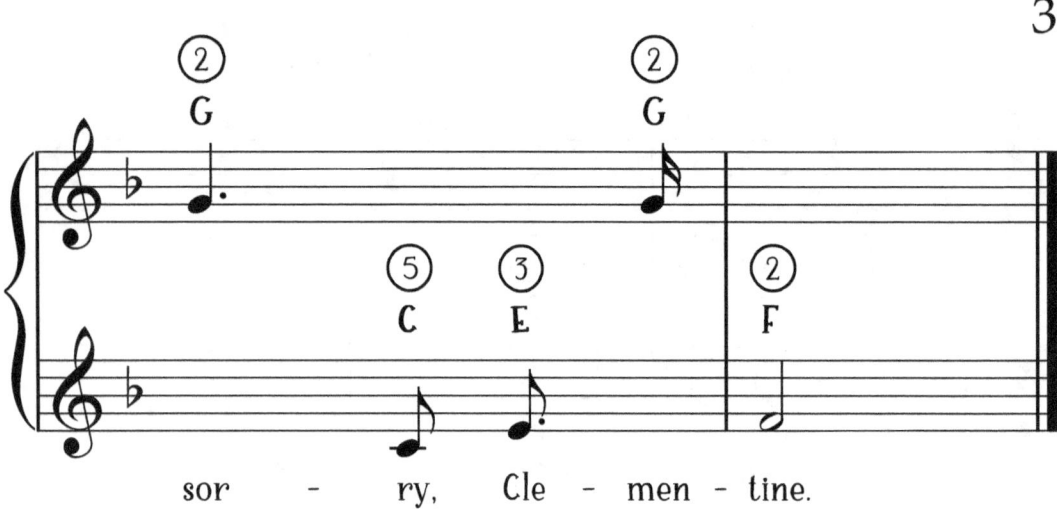

sor - ry, Cle - men - tine.

2. Light she was and like a feather,
   And her shoes were number nine.
   Herring boxes without topses,
   Sandals were for Clementine.

   Refrain

3. Drove she ducklings to the water,
   Every morning just at nine,
   Hit her foot against a splinter,
   Fell into the foaming brine.

   Refrain

4. Ruby lips above the water,
   Blowing bubbles soft and fine,
   Alas for me! I was no swimmer,
   So I lost my Clementine.

   Refrain

MIDDLE
C
F# Gb G# Ab A# Bb C# Db D# Eb F# Gb G# Ab A# Bb C# Db D# Eb
F G A B C D E F G A B C D E

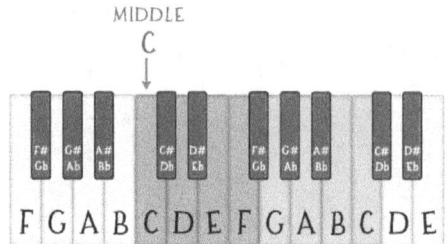

Helpful tip at the end of the song!

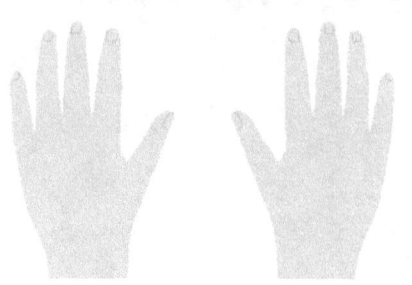

BUFFALO GALS

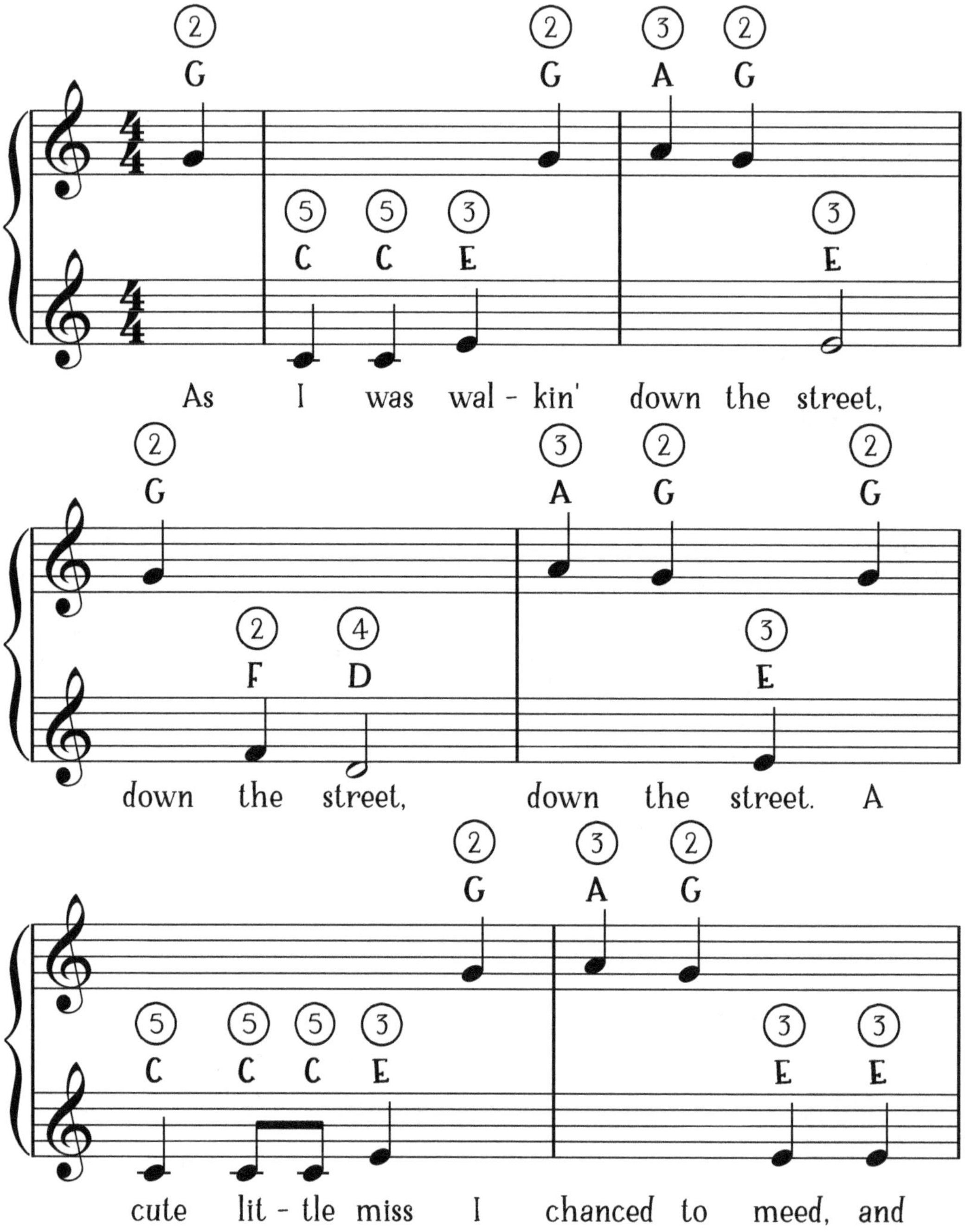

2 G 2 G 3 A 2 G
5 C 5 C 3 E 3 E
As I was wal - kin' down the street,
2 G 3 A 2 G 2 G
2 F 4 D 3 E
down the street, down the street. A
2 G 3 A 2 G
5 C 5 C 5 C 3 E 3 E 3 E
cute lit - tle miss I chanced to meed, and

3

5 5 4 3 2 2
C C B A G G
Buf - fa - lo Gals won't you
3 2 2 5 5
A G G C C
3
E
come out to - night, won't you
4 2 2
B G G
2 2 4 5
F F D C
dance by the light of the moon.

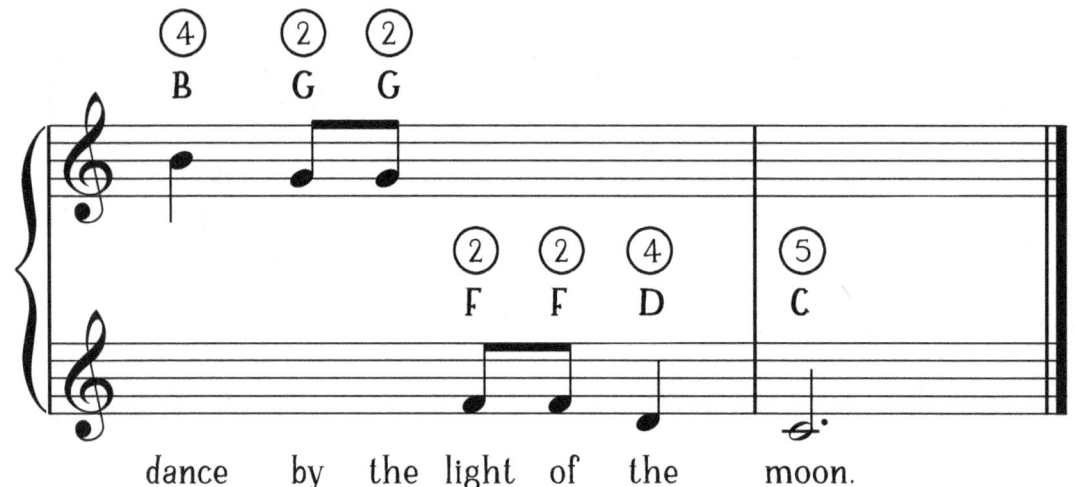

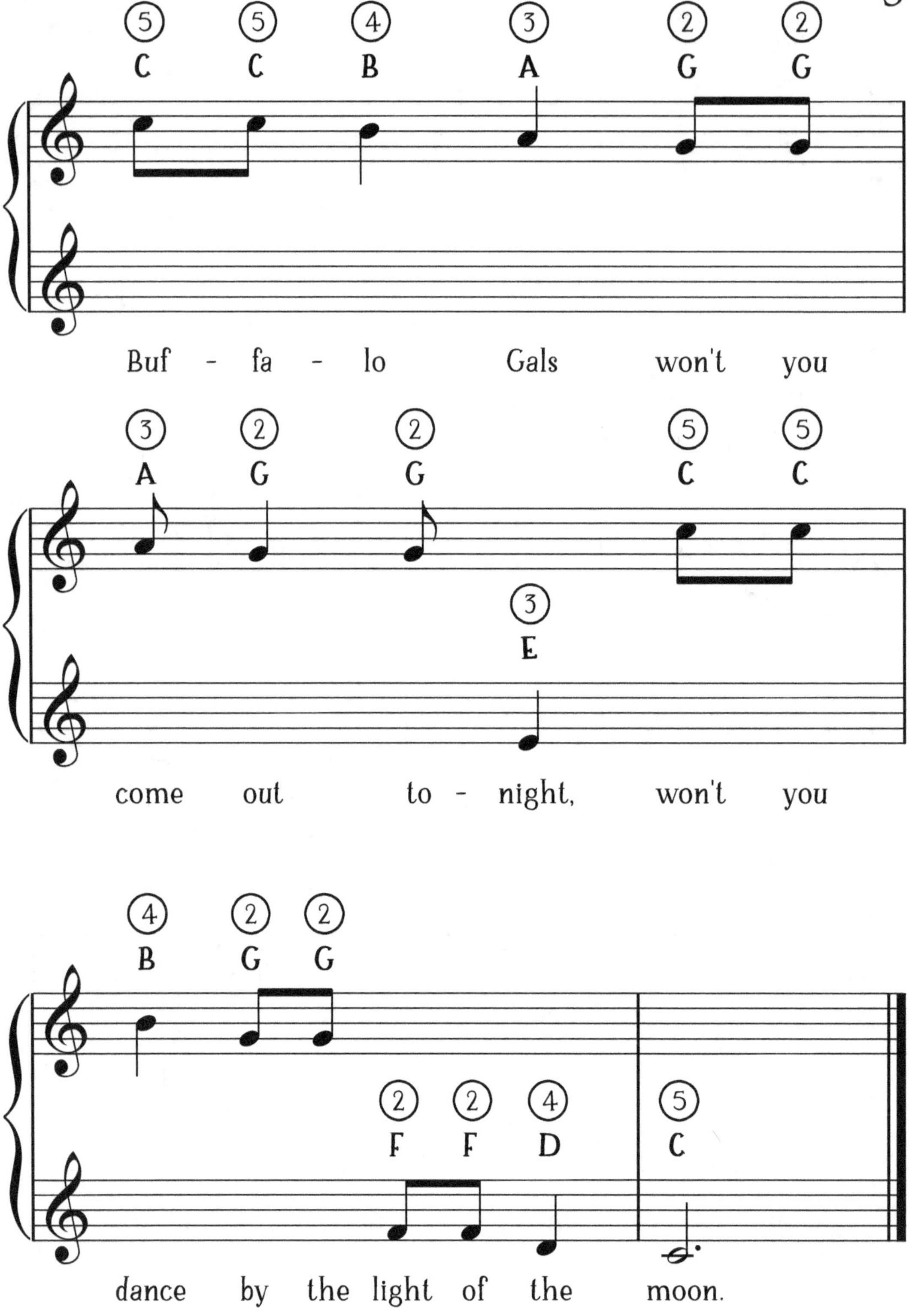

2. I asked her would she have some talk,
   Have some talk, have some talk.
   Her feet covered the whole sidewalk
   As she stood close by me.

3. I asked her would she have a dance,
   Have a dance, have a dance.
   I thought I might get a chance
   To shake a foot with her.

4. I'd like to make that gal my wife,
   Gal my wife, gal my wife.
   I'd be happy all my life.
   If I had her by me.

TIP

This song will introduce you to a new rhythm. It is called syncopation. There should always be a shorter note, followed by a note at least twice as long. This sounds as if the accent is placed a bit later than it should be.

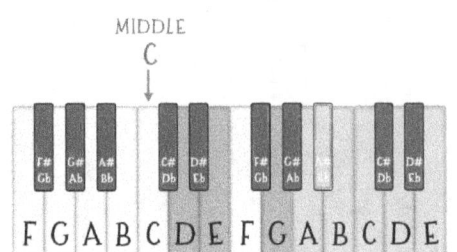

Helpful tip at the end of the song!

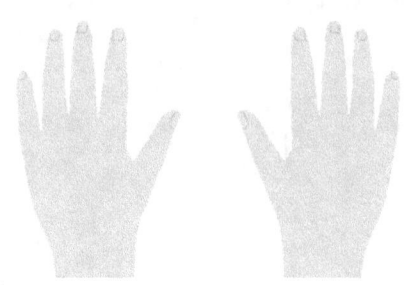

JOHN JACOB JINGLEHEIMER SCHMIDT

John   Ja - cob   Jin-gle-hei-mer Schmidt,   His name   is   my   name   too,   When ev - er   we   go   out,   the

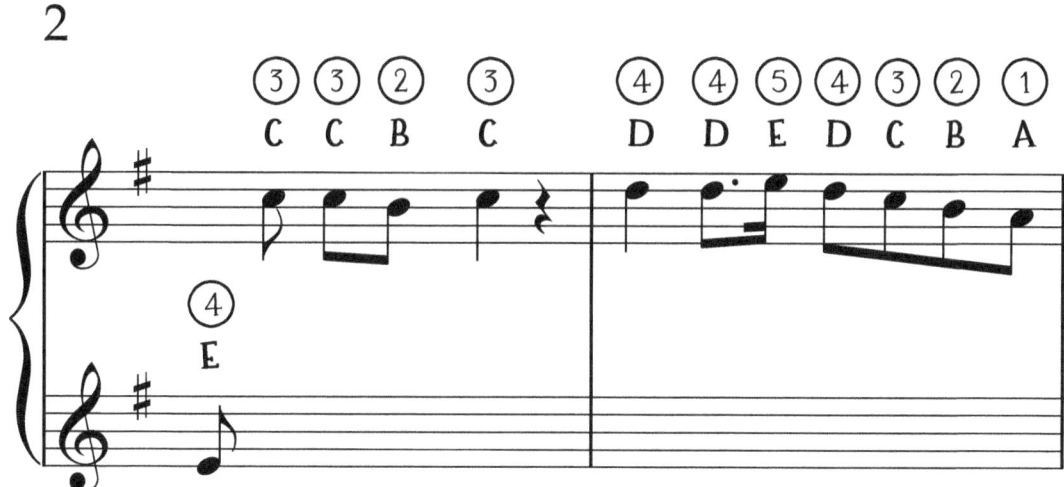
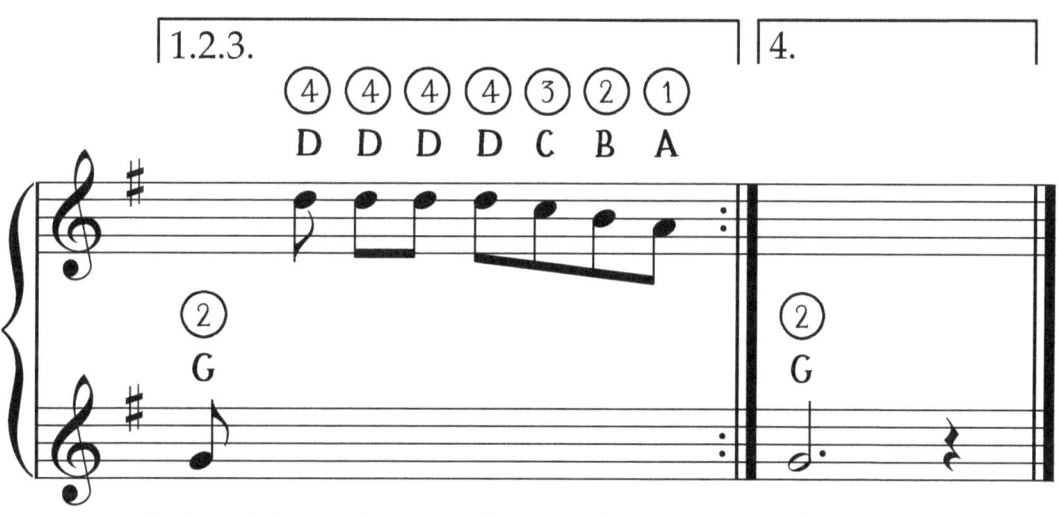

 TIP

In some songs, you need to repeat parts in a particular way. Look at the illustration below, you'll see the signs that will tell you what parts and how many times you need to repeat each of them.

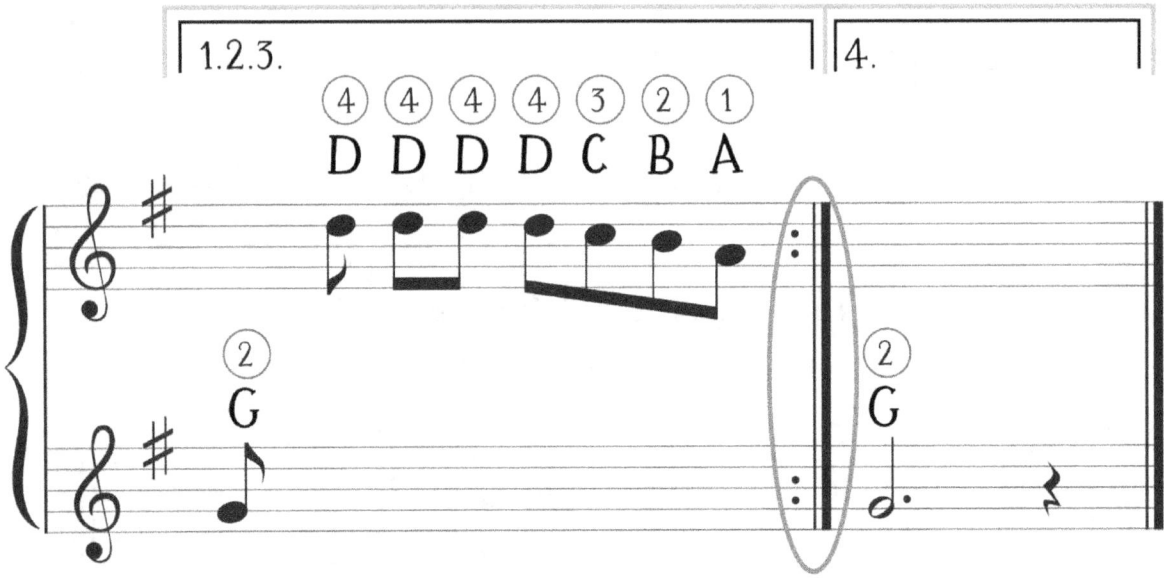

- The circle shows a reprise sign. When you get to it, you should start playing the song from the beginning.

- The two open boxes with numbers above the staff are called Volta brackets. They will tell you how many times you need to repeat a section.

In this song, for example, you repeat the first part three times in total (the section that is before the reprise sing.) Then, on the fourth time, you play the same part again, but skip everything inside the 1.2.3. Volta bracket and just play the fourth part instead.

MIDDLE C
F# Gb G# Ab A# Bb C# Db D# Eb F# Gb G# Ab A# Bb C# Db D# Eb
F G A B C D E F G A B C D E

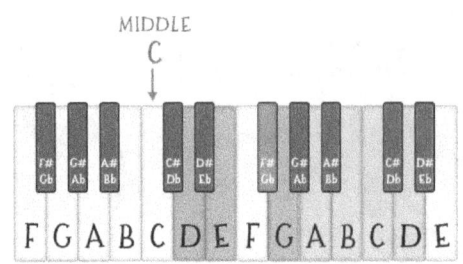

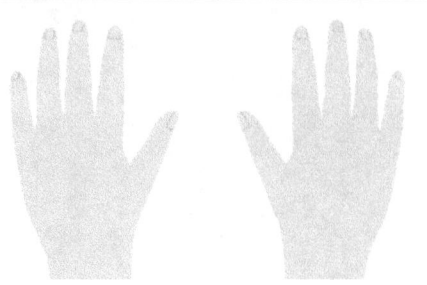

MY GRANFATHER'S CLOCK

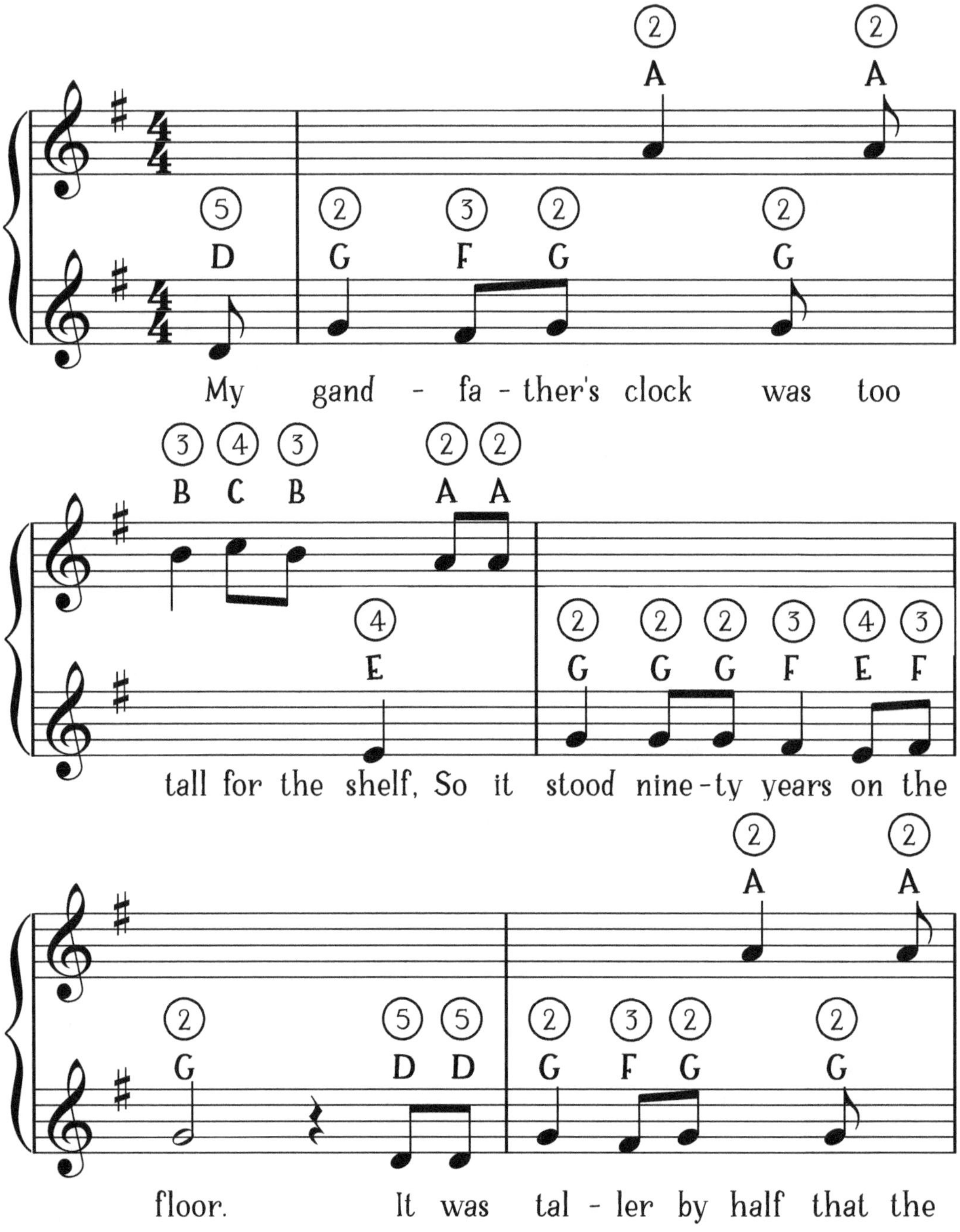

A A
D G F G G
My gand - fa - ther's clock was too
B C B A A
E G G G F E F
tall for the shelf, So it stood nine-ty years on the
A A
G D D G F G G
floor. It was tal - ler by half that the

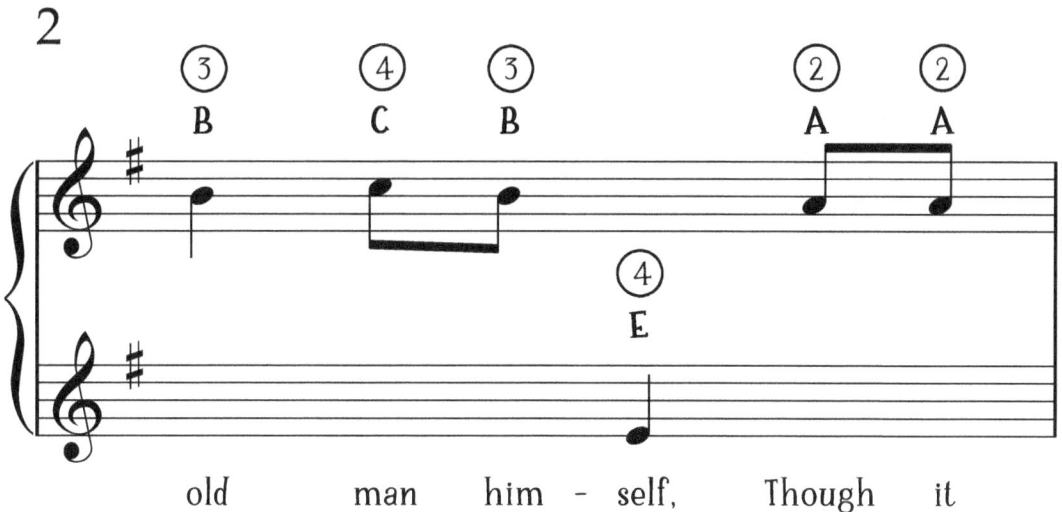
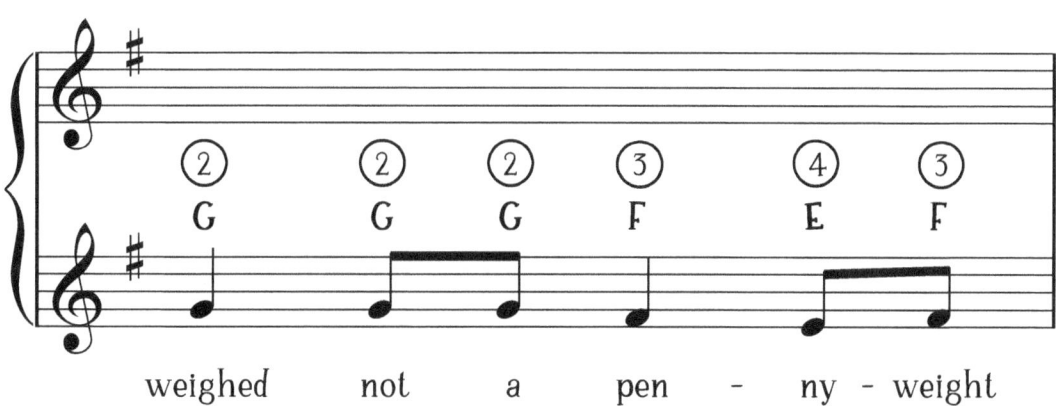

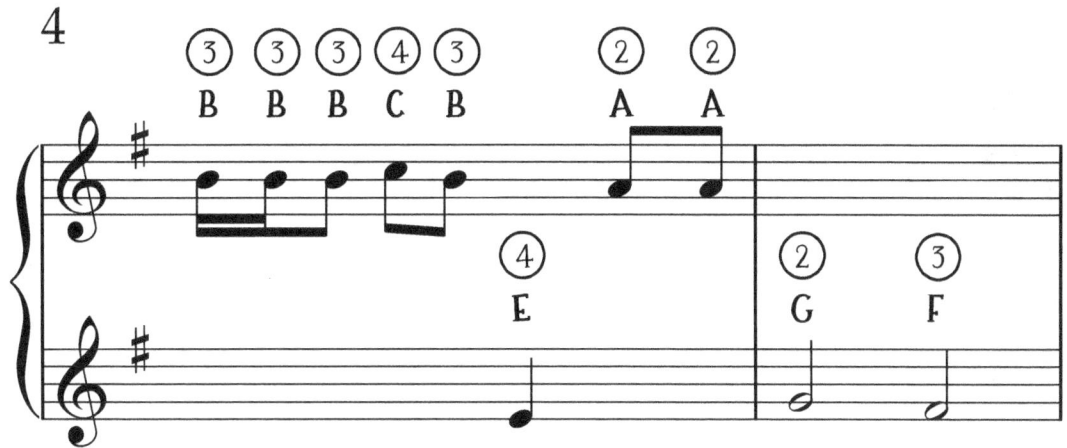
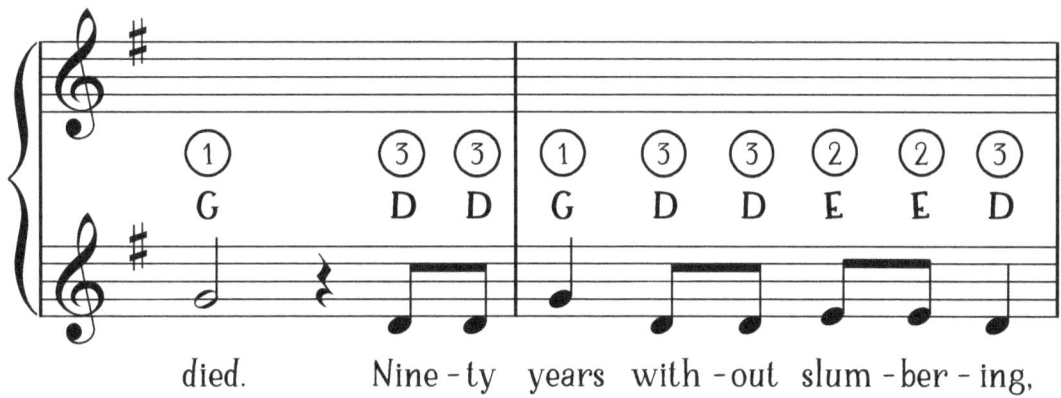
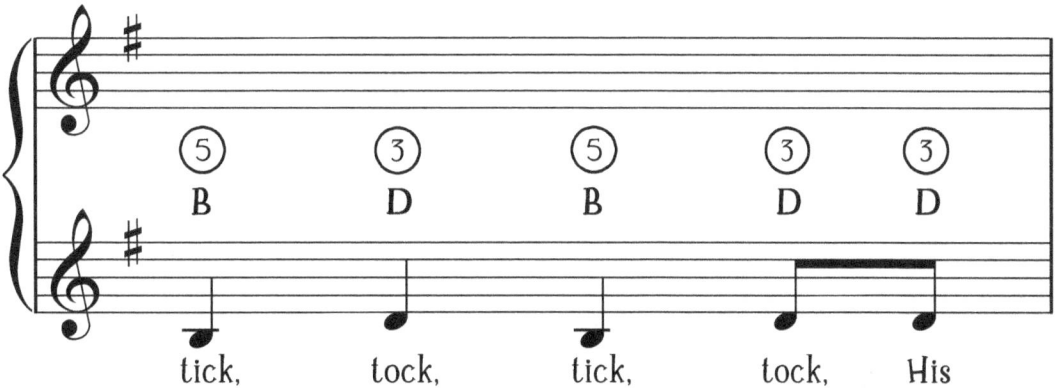

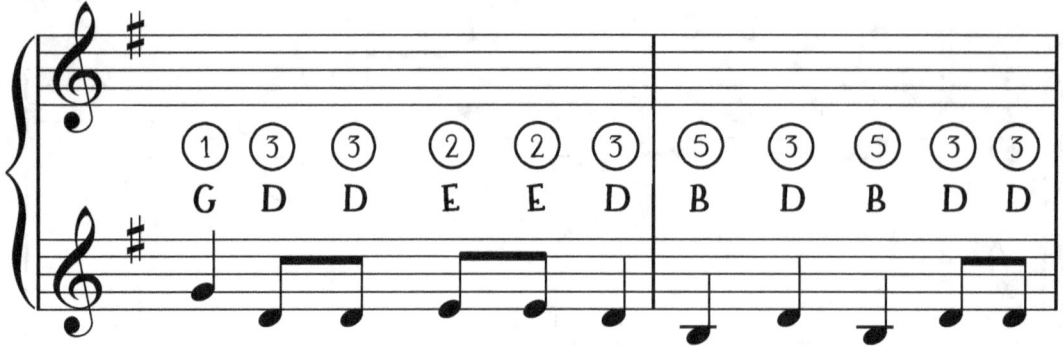

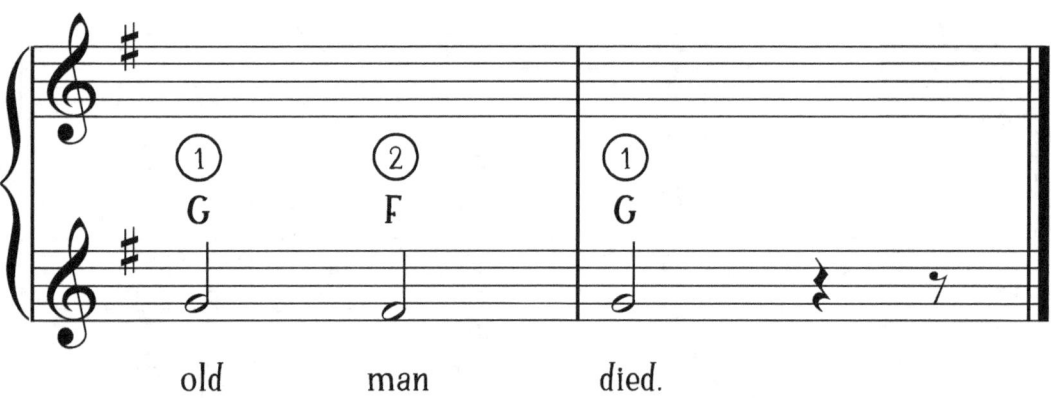

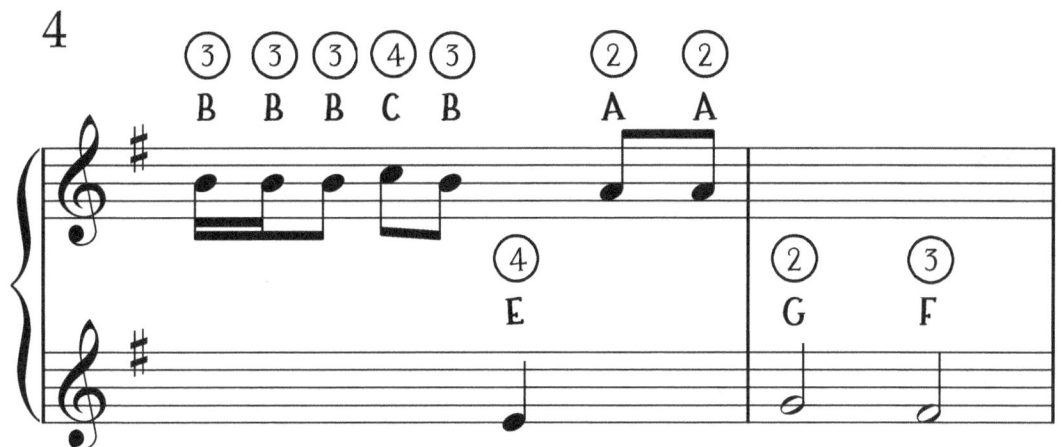
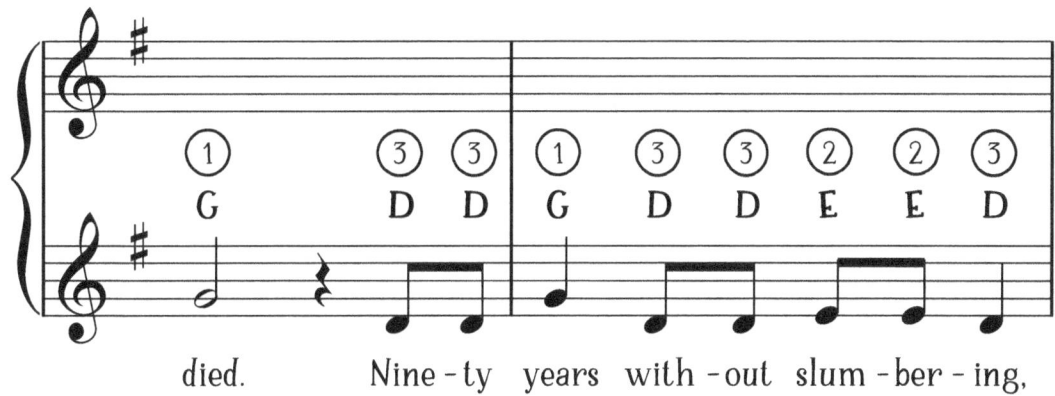
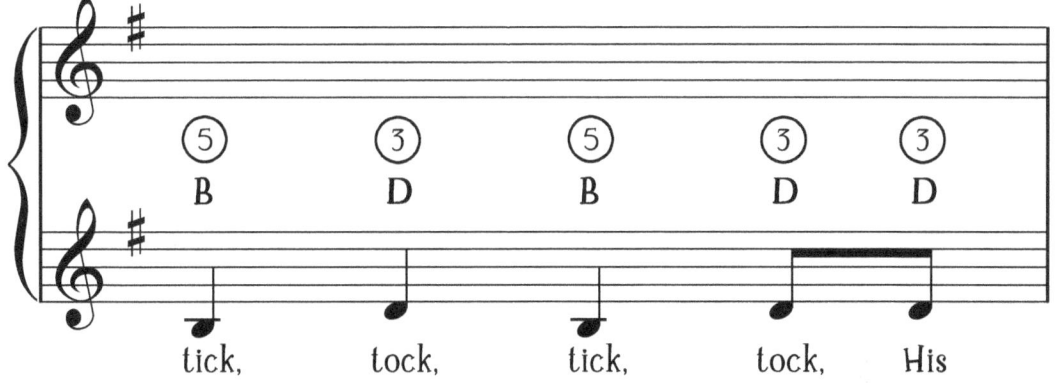

5

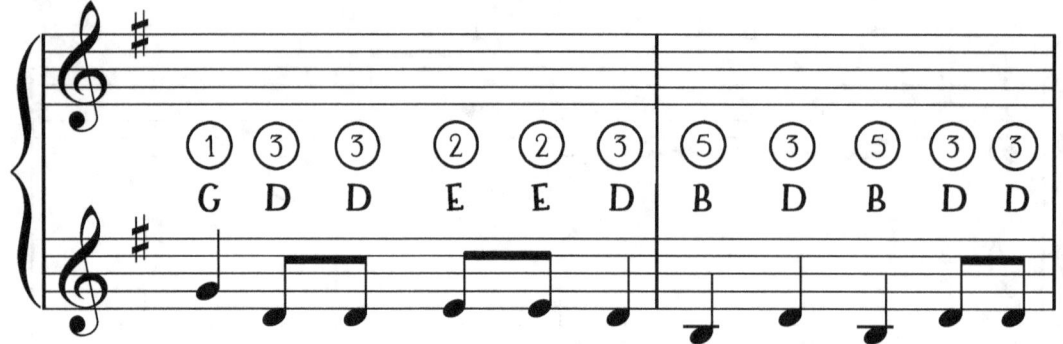

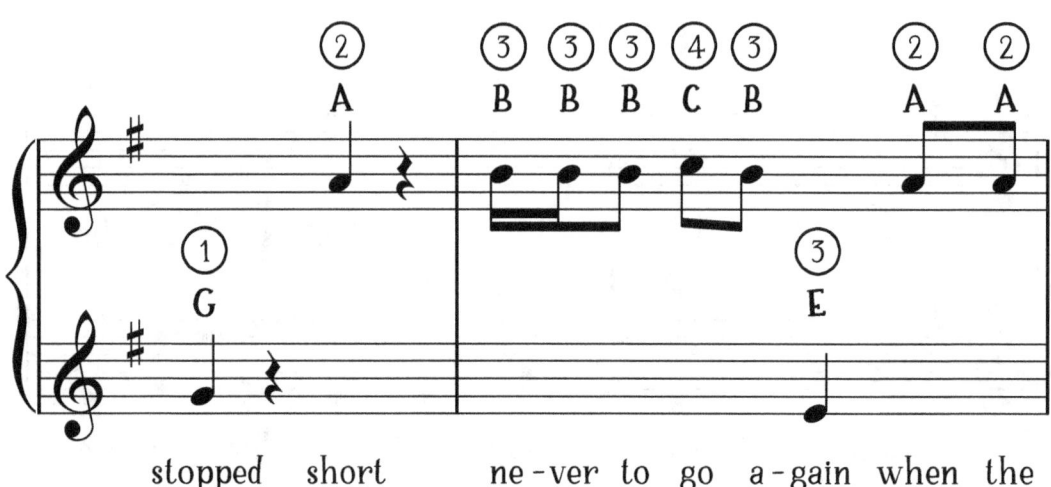

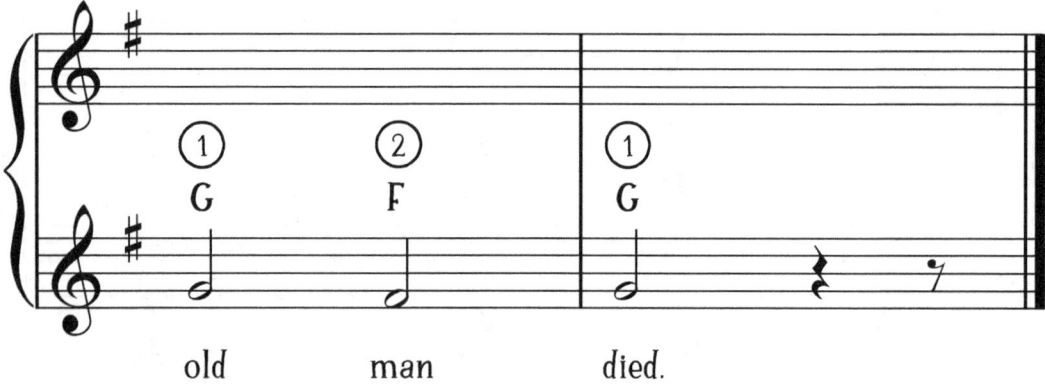

CONCLUSION

As we come to the end of this musical journey together, I want to thank all of you for your hard work and excitement in learning about the wonderful world of piano music. I've enjoyed helping you navigate this fun journey through 50 songs, from well-known songs like "Hot Cross Buns" and "Itsy Bitsy Spider" to fun rhythmic songs like "Bow Wow Wow" and "If You're Happy and You Know It." You've learned how to play these themes and also how sharps, flats, dotted rhythms, and repeat signs can be used to make music more interesting. I hope that each practice lesson has helped you learn new things and understand how music works. As you close this book, remember that your path through music isn't over—it's an adventure that lasts a lifetime. Check out more songs, play around with different rhythms, and enjoy the process of making music. Keep practicing, keep learning, and above all, keep playing with love and curiosity.

Happy playing!

SPECIAL BONUS!

Want These 2 Books For FREE?

Get **FREE**, unlimited access to these and all of our new kids books by joining our community!

Scan W/ Your Camera To Join!

www.ingramcontent.com/pod-product-compliance
Lightning Source LLC
Chambersburg PA
CBHW081618100526
44590CB00021B/3492